The Political Economy of Land Degradation

Pressure Groups, Foreign Aid and the Myth of Man-Made Deserts

Julian Morris

Published by the
IEA Environment Unit

1995

First published in May 1995
by

THE ENVIRONMENT UNIT
THE INSTITUTE OF ECONOMIC AFFAIRS
2 Lord North Street, Westminster,
London SW1P 3LB

Studies on the Environment No.5

ISBN 0-255 36348-6

Cover design by David Lucas

Typography by Stuart Blade Enterprises

Set in Plantin and Univers
Printed in Great Britain by
Goron Pro-Print Co Ltd, Lancing, W. Sussex

Table of Contents

Foreword

The idea of desertification is a sitting target for an IEA study. Desertification sits there by virtue of its inherent imperfection as a notion and its curious persistence among a stolid multinational system of functionaries who, though individually sceptical, have been unable collectively to bring the system to its senses. The concept of desertification has never, since it surfaced in the 1940s, been properly thought out, but despite continual censure, it has bounced along the bottom of the scientific and bureaucratic consciousness without ever being squashed out of existence.

This obduracy has several reasons. Despite being a very bad scientific concept, because it is virtually unmeasurable, the venal fringe of the scientific community has been attracted by the promise of cash from governments and international agencies. Scientific definitions, however, are inevitably arbitrary: where is the edge of the desert? what is a desert? Deserts are unavoidably constructs, economic, social or individual, depending for greater precision on the supplies of capital, initiative and labour, and perceptions and abilities to withstand risk (or the scientist's perception of how to make a quick and dirty compromise to get his report in on time). It may have been a good bureaucratic mealticket in the short term, but the failures to deliver among the UN bodies, which Julian Morris describes, show that it has brought the longer-term reputations of some agencies into serious question.

It is because Julian Morris has captured the essence of this sorry story that I am happy to write a foreword to his booklet. I have to admit and, where appropriate, apologise for my part in the slide from the slippery edge of concern in the early 1970s into the deep quagmire of confusion in the mid 1980s. I joined the gravy train when I was recruited to write one of four background documents of the World Conference on Desertification (held in Nairobi in 1977). My research quickly bewildered me, and I hope that I was able to spell out the reasons for my bemusement. I got back on the bandwagon with two further reports. In some of these, I dare say that I was as blind as many of my desertification colleagues, but I can point to passages in which I believe I pinpointed some of the pitfalls that are now all too apparent. None of the reports, at least, was as simplistic as UNEP's disastrously flawed *World Atlas of Desertification*, which, despite some fair attempts at regional analysis, must be regarded as the apogee of the confusion about desertification.

The worst sufferers from this kind of disarray have undoubtedly been the inhabitants of the dry lands themselves. Unlike the clients of professionals in most countries, they have not been able to fire those who have given bad advice. Indeed the advisors have bounced back even more quickly than their concepts. The dry world still contains more than its share of the poor, and certainly more than its share of the poorest countries. Despite the lack of good evidence, I believe that their problems do have something to do with their environment. The evidence is poor largely because of the complexity of the issues. Having been mired in environmental problems, people in the dry lands become subject to a downward spiral of civil and international conflict, debt, disease, and so on. Interrelatedness and complexity have been swept from sight by the momentum of the simplistic desertification concept. I agree with Julian Morris that these complexities are better dealt with by individuals on the unforgiving ground than by distant, comfortable, too often forgiven 'experts'.

Julian Morris's study, I am glad to say, is on the crest of a new wave of studies looking at the problems of dry lands, though the new consciousness is only now beginning to penetrate to the dignitaries. There have been some excellent reports among these, of which Tiffen, Mortimore and Gichuki's report on Machakos in Kenya, given some prominence by the present study, is the most thought-provoking. The main lesson from these studies is not so much that degradation is or is not occurring, but more that agricultural economies in the dry parts of the world are immensely complex. As Julian Morris says, the wet world has made many of the judgements that have counted about the dry lands in the last few centuries, and in looking in from the outside

7

we have inevitably oversimplified. The ways in which the dry world reaches prosperity will be at least as complex as the ways in which the rest of us have reached it (if we have), and, because of their vastly more unpredictable environment, may well have to be even more complicated. Above all, it will be ways that they discover (as in Machakos) rather than ways in which they are ordered to do so.

I hope and believe that Julian Morris's study will provoke a more informed debate about how the drylands should feature in our view of the future. It comes at a good time, as the secretariat of the new Convention on Desertification tries to rescue some credibility for the 'world community' out of the chaos of the last two decades. I particularly like his conclusion, where he displays a refreshingly new view of the issues. I hope, above all, that it will put one more (but unfortunately not the last) nail in the coffin of the concept of desertification, which has served us all so badly.

April 1995   ANDREW WARREN
                                           University College, London

Dr Andrew Warren *is Lecturer in Geography at University College, London. He has published widely on problems of land degradation and on geomorphology. He is co-author of a 1988 report on desertification for Greenpeace, and also a 1992 report on land degradation for the United Nations Development Programme.*

Preface

As Andrew Warren and Julian Morris have eloquently exposed, desertification has been the quintessential United Nations programme; the supreme gravy train for Western consultants.

A recent investigation into the UN's 'integrity, efficiency and cost effectiveness' commissioned by the Secretary-General, Mr Boutros Boutros Ghali, reported that the UN 'is almost totally lacking in effective means to deal with fraud, waste and abuse by staff'. Julian Morris carefully explains how these problems have affected the functioning of the United Nations Environment Programme (UNEP).

The IEA Environment Unit is delighted to offer this paper on desertification and the political economy of land degradation. The views expressed are of course those of the author, not of the Institute (which has no corporate view), its Trustees, Advisers or Directors.

April 1995   ROGER BATE
                              Director, IEA Environment Unit

The Author

Julian Morris has an MA in Economics from Edinburgh University, an MSc in Environmental and Resource Economics from University College, London, and is currently pursuing a PhD at Cambridge University. He has worked as an econometrician for Commerzbank in Frankfurt, and as a consultant to the National Foundation for Teaching Entrepreneurship (UK), the World Wide Fund for Nature and Save the Rhino International.

Mr Morris became a Research Fellow of the IEA Environment Unit in November 1993 and was a Summer Research Fellow at the Atlas Economic Research Foundation in 1994.

In March 1994, the IEA Environment Unit published *Global Warming: Apocalypse or Hot Air?*, which Mr Morris co-authored with Roger Bate.

Acknowledgements

A great many people have helped bring this paper to fruition: Patrick Darling, Roger Bate, Lorraine Mooney, and two anonymous referees provided helpful comments on earlier versions; Andrew Warren proffered an abundance of corrections and comments and wrote a wonderful foreword; the Institute of Economic Affairs and the Atlas Economic Research Foundation supplied financial support and technical assistance; Colin Robinson edited out many imperfections; Lisa Mac Lellan decoded my awful handwriting; John Blundell continued to believe, against evidence to the contrary, that I would finally get something written; Alejandro Chafuen, Jo Ann Kwong, Carl Helstrom and all the staff at Atlas provided support during my 1994 summer fellowship; Walter Grinder, Bill Beach, Mark Brady, Elaine Hawley and the Summer Fellows at the Institute for Humane Studies at George Mason University provided much needed intellectual stimuli and friendship; and Melissa English tempered my emotions and reassured me that sanity was just around the corner. The usual caveat applies.

J.M.

Introduction

'And in the seven plenteous years the earth brought forth by handfuls. ...
And Joseph gathered corn ...
And the seven years of plenteousness, that was in the land of Egypt, was
   ended.
And the seven years of dearth began to come ...
   And Joseph opened all the storehouses, and sold unto the Egyptians.'
                              (Attrib. Moses, *Genesis*, ch. 41, vs. 47-56)

For all of history the lands bordering deserts have been prone to drought, their inhabitants frequently threatened with starvation. Yet people have lived, indeed thrived, under such conditions – overcoming the threat of starvation by establishing customs, traditions and trade, and by inventing new technologies and institutions.

Equally persistent, however, has been the fear, expressed most eloquently and vociferously by persons living far from the desert fringes, that the desert dweller, acting out of stupidity and ignorance, is destroying the very means of his[1] subsistence. This fear, exacerbated over the past 25 years by media reports of famine in Africa and the recent spate of apocalyptic environmental doomsaying, has firmly established the myth of man-made deserts.[2] Officials at the United Nations, encouraged by the media hype, have called for massive funding of 'anti-desertification' activities: in 1992, Mostafa Tolba, then executive director of the United Nations Environment Programme (UNEP), claimed that up to $480 billion must be spent over the next 20

---

[1] As de Jasay (1989, p.1) suggests, 'wherever I say "he" or "man", I really mean "she" or "woman"'.

[2] A number of people have pointed out that the use of the word *myth* here may cause some confusion, so I will attempt to clarify my position from the outset: some deserts may owe their existence principally to human action, but, as the evidence presented in Chapter 2 indicates, most are the product of 'natural' (that is, not human) causes. The *myth* is that a significant proportion of the world's desert land is the consequence of human action.

years in order to 'arrest' the 'global threat of desertification'. In October 1994, officials from 87 nation states met in Paris to sign the Convention on Desertification, which obliges the governments of developed nations to provide 'significant financial resources' to the governments of developing nations – ostensibly to be spent on 'anti-desertification' projects.

Drawing on a diverse literature, this paper presents a critical assessment of the theory underpinning the United Nations Convention on Desertification. The work is divided into two parts. Part One begins with a brief history of the ideologies and interventions which have led to the Convention on Desertification. This is followed by a discussion of the evidence for and against a number of competing theories which seek to explain the evolution of deserts and the causes of desertification. Part Two begins with a very brief overview of the political economy of Africa. This is followed by an explanation of the root causes of land degradation and some tentative proposals for resolving the related problems of poverty, hunger and land degradation in the developing world. An appendix discusses the problem of land degradation in the United States.

PART I

The Myth of Man-Made Deserts

1. Ideology and Intervention

Ancient Greece

As far back as the 5th century BC, Plato lamented the degeneration of his civilisation: Attica[1] was no longer cultivated 'by true husbandmen, who made husbandry their business, and were lovers of honour, and of a noble nature' (Plato, *Critias*, cited by Wall, 1994, pp.36-7). As a result, Attica had become deforested, the soils depleted: 'there are remaining only the bones of the wasted body...all the richer and softer parts of the soil having fallen away.'[2] Plato's proposed solution was the creation of a rationally constructed polis, in which all action would be guided by the dictates of a philosopher-king (Plato, 1955).

Colonial Africa and Asia

More recently, David Livingstone, travelling through the arid lands of southern Africa in the 1850s, suggested that the desert-like conditions he observed might be the result of a gradual drying-up, a 'progressive desiccation',[3] of the land (Livingstone, 1857). These ideas were reiterated in the early part of this century by Schwartz (1919, 1921) who, concerned that the process was still occurring, proposed, 'Grandiose schemes to divert rivers and flood depressions' (Thomas & Middleton, 1994, p.19) as a means of reversing the process. However, 'a

---

[1] Attica was the eastern-central district of ancient Greece, whose capital was Athens.

[2] Recent research indicates that erosion of the hills of ancient Greece did coincide with human habitation (van Andel *et al.*, 1990), but there is no evidence to support the claim that 'true husbandmen' ever existed.

[3] As Thomas and Middleton (1994, p.19) explain:

'The concept of post-glacial "progressive desiccation" was based upon the twin tenets that wet conditions characterised the glacial phases of the Pleistocene [from 2,500,000 to 10,000 years ago – that is, until the end of the last ice age] and that aridity had increased since the warming of the ice sheets in the Holocene [10,000 years ago to the present day].'

government commission sent to the Kalahari to investigate in 1925 cast doubt on the validity of the ideas and the evidence used to back them up' (Thomas & Middleton, 1994, p.19), and Schwartz's proposals were not enacted.

From the turn of the century, progressive desiccation became an explanation for all manner of phenomena. Travellers told of how Asian nomads, having lost their lands to the expanding desert, were forced to invade neighbouring pastures (Thomas & Middleton, 1994). Bovill (1921) asserted that declining yields on Sahelian and West African fields were the result of the 'encroachment of the Sahara', a problem which Stebbing (1935) saw as a 'threat to the West African colonies'.[4] But Bovill acknowledged that other researchers disagreed with his assessment (he even cited a report which suggested that sub-Saharan Africa might be becoming wetter). Moreover, an Anglo-French forestry commission sent to investigate the situation was unable to find any evidence of progressive desiccation or large-scale sand movement (Dregne & Tucker, 1987, p.17).

During the 1930s, primarily as a result of the emergence of the 'Dust Bowl'[5] in the American West, Plato's paradigm came back into vogue: land degradation was seen as the result of poor husbandry and could only be mitigated through the imposition of a central authority controlling land use. At a dinner of the Royal African Society, the president, the Earl of Athlone (1938), commented:

> 'That this council views with the gravest concern the widespread destruction of the African soil by erosion consequent on wasteful methods of husbandry which strike at the basis of rural economy and Native welfare, and is of the opinion that immediate steps should be taken for the adoption of common policy and energetic measures throughout British Africa in order to put an effective check upon this growing menace to the true fertility of the land and to the health of its inhabitants.'

---

[4] Dregne and Tucker (1987) note that 'Stebbing quoted a French political officer who served in Niger and Mali as saying that the Sahara had advanced toward the south at a rate of 1 km per year for the past 300 years'.

[5] This was the name given, by a Washington newspaper, to the region of the Great Plains which suffered severe drought and wind erosion in the 1930s. For a discussion of the creation and perpetuation of land degradation in the American West, see the Appendix (below, pp.91-93).

In case concern for 'Native welfare' was insufficient motivation to take action, Lord Dufferin, speaking at the same dinner, appealed to his audience's self-interest:

'The subject that we are going to discuss tonight is one of the very greatest importance not merely to our Colonial Empire and not merely to Africa, but to the whole of the World...'

In this case, the philosopher-king was to be the colonial agriculturist, whose attitude is eloquently expressed by the following passage from the 1945 Annual Report of the Kenyan Agricultural Department:

'The African in Kenya has not yet arrived at the level of education which enables him ... to plan his agricultural economy successfully ... In his case, therefore, it is essential that his general farming policy shall, to a large extent, be dictated to him in the light of the experience and knowledge of officers of Government responsible for his welfare...' (quoted by Tiffen *et al.*, 1994, p.252).

Singled out for treatment was the Machakos district of Kenya, of which Colin Maher wrote in 1937:

'The Machakos Reserve is an appalling example of ... uncoordinated and practically uncontrolled development by natives whose multiplication and the increase of whose stock has been permitted, free from the checks of war and largely from those of disease, under benevolent British rule'(quoted by Tiffen *et al.*, 1994, p.3).

Independence and the Rise of the UN

Following independence, many people in the 'developed' world continued to promote the belief in impending ecological doom in the 'developing' world. These concerns were voiced through the many institutions involved in 'development', the most active of which were the various United Nations (UN) offshoots.[6]

---

[6] In 1951, the directors of the United Nations Educational, Scientific and Cultural Organisation (UNESCO) set up an 'arid lands programme'. By 1958 this had become one of UNESCO's largest projects, and was subsequently expanded still further through the inclusion of semi-arid lands. The directors of the Food and Agriculture Organisation (FAO) of the UN soon established links with UNESCO's arid lands programme, providing soil analyses and giving 'expert' advice on appropriate

Towards the end of the 1960s, a number of authors began to reiterate the Malthusian concerns raised by the colonial agriculturists: that populations in developing countries were expanding more rapidly than the means of sustenance (for example, Boulding, 1966). In 1967, the directors of the UN, with the support of the US Department of State and the United States Agency for International Development (USAID), responded to this purported threat by setting up the Fund for Population Activities (UNFPA). The UNFPA exists primarily as a financial conduit to 'projects designed to curb population growth in all continents' (Kasun, 1988, p.199).

In 1971, at the height of one of the worst droughts the Sahel[7] has experienced this century, the 'encroaching Sahara' theory was resuscitated. At a UN Seminar on the Environment and Development an official from the USAID mission in Tunisia asserted the importance of keeping the 'northward march of the Sahara' in check. In the subsequent USAID report, an official claimed that 'there has been a net advance in some places along a 2,000-mile southern front [of the Sahara] of as much as 30 miles a year' (USAID, 1972). In June 1972, the UN held a 'Conference on the Human Environment' in Stockholm, and subsequently set up the United Nations Environment Program (UNEP). At its first session in June 1973, the Governing Council of UNEP requested that its executive director, Mostafa Tolba, mount a concerted programme to 'arrest' the spread of deserts and to 'help countries in mitigating the consequences of drought'.[8] In December of that same year, UNEP's Governing Council set up the Permanent Inter-State Committee on Drought Control in the Sahel (CILSS), which was to be responsible for conducting, 'a viable drought control programme, thereby attempting to alleviate human suffering due to drought, bringing

---

agricultural techniques. The directors of the World Meteorological Office (WMO) were likewise happy to associate themselves with UNESCO's arid lands programme, carrying out research into climatic conditions in 'afflicted' countries (Odingo, 1990).

[7] The Sahel is the semi-arid region on the Southern fringes of the Sahara desert extending across West Africa, from Senegal to the border of the Sudan.

[8] This was part of UN General Assembly Resolution 3054 (XXVIII) (Odingo, 1990, pp.31-33).

science and technology to "fight" drought and to rehabilitate drought-damaged land in the Sahel' (Odingo, 1990, p.31).[9]

Preparing for the War

The UN began to prepare its 'armies' for the 'war' against the deserts in 1974. The Governing Council of the United Nations Development Programme (UNDP) 'called for the need to undertake in-depth studies on the extent of the drought in Africa and to draw up corresponding action programmes' (Odingo, 1990, p.34). The UN General Assembly (29th session) called for 'international action to combat desertification' and announced that a Conference on Desertification (UNCOD) would be held in 1977 so as 'to give impetus to [this] international action to combat desertification' (Odingo, 1990, p.34). A new organ was created by the UN General Assembly: the United Nations Sudano-Sahelian Office (UNSO) was to act as a conduit for the Trust Fund for Sudano-Sahelian Activities, 'providing assistance to governments in planning and co-ordination of ... projects of crucial importance to the recovery and rehabilitation of the Sahel and for combating desertification' (UNSO, 1990).

By the end of 1974, at least nine UN organisations were directly involved in the 'war' against the expanding deserts. Underlying all this activity was the assumption that through some as yet undefined process, called 'desertification',[10] deserts

---

[9] Odingo (1990) notes that 'The way CILSS was conceptualised reveals assumptions of scientific and technical "superiority" over environmental problems like drought, by suggesting that all the "armaments" were available for the "war" against drought, and that what was now important was to work out a "battle" plan' (p.33). He ascribes this use of militaristic language such as 'fight' and 'combat' to the technocratic approach taken by UNEP about environmental problems in general: 'Many of the proposed activities were guided by the false assumption that technology had the answer to all the problems being addressed. Over the years, this assumption influenced the language used which was clearly unrealistic, words such as to "combat", to "stop" and to "reverse"' (p.31).

[10] The term 'desertification' was originally used by Aubreville (1949) to mean the creation of deserts in tropical (that is, humid) regions: the removal of indigenous trees and excessive cultivation (by the marauding Natives) of nutrient-weak soil was leading to soil erosion, which Aubreville supposed would eventually lead to the creation of deserts via edaphic (soil) desiccation. However, it is clear that UNEP wished to be less specific – there has even been an odd debate raging over whether 'desertification' is a process or a state (Glantz & Orlovsky, 1984).

were expanding and thereby threatening the livelihoods of the people living on their fringes.

UNCOD and Beyond

At the 1977 United Nations Conference on Desertification (UNCOD) an *official definition of desertification* was announced:

> 'Desertification is the diminution or destruction of the biological potential of the land, and can lead ultimately to desert-like conditions. It is an aspect of the widespread deterioration of ecosystems and has diminished or destroyed the biological potential for multiple use purposes at a time when increased productivity is needed to support growing populations in quest of development' (Odingo, 1990, p.36).

Despite the vague nature of this definition (see chapter 2 on the semantics of desertification), the delegates at UNCOD agreed on a Plan of Action to Combat Desertification (the PACD), whose 28 recommendations embrace three central objectives (Thomas & Middleton, 1994, p.31):

- to stop and reverse desertification processes,

- to establish sustainable land practices,

- to support the social and economic development of population groups directly affected by desertification.

The director-general of UNEP, Mostafa Tolba, was given responsibility for co-ordinating the PACD,[11] and the UN General Assembly voted to create another three bodies, under the auspices of which UNEP's officials would carry out their plans:

- The *Desertification Branch*, subsequently renamed the Desertification Control Programme Activity Centre *(DC/PAC)*, is the overseer of day-to-day operations;

- The *Consultative Group for Desertification Control (DESCON)* is responsible for promoting awareness of the

---

[11] Thomas & Middleton (1994, pp.35-36) note that UNEP was probably not the most appropriate institution to carry out the PACD.

desertification 'issue' and for co-ordinating the activities of other UN organisations in the war against desertification;

• The *Inter-Agency Working Group on Desertification (IAWGD)* facilitates co-ordination between relevant UN bodies.[12]

Following UNCOD, these agencies spent huge sums of money on anti-desertification projects, desertification monitoring systems, reports and conferences (see below, Chapter 5).

Another severe drought in 1984 kept the 'encroaching Sahara' theory in the public eye. In addition, a few outspoken scientists and pressure groups began to warn of imminent global warming (see below, Chapter 3) and catastrophic losses of biological diversity. In response to the conventional wisdom that 'something must be done' about all these scary scenarios, UN officials nominated themselves the saviours of the Earth.

'The Earth Summit'

In December 1989, the UN General Assembly passed resolution 44/228, which called for a Conference on Environment and Development (UNCED) to be held in June 1992 in Brazil (*The Earth Summit*, 1993, p.3). Along the way, the Preparatory Committee met four times: in Nairobi, Geneva (twice) and New York. The principal objective of these meetings was to formulate Agenda 21, the aim of which is explained by UNCED secretary-general Maurice Strong:

> 'Agenda 21 would go well beyond the kind of 'Action Plans' which have emerged from UN conferences. It should provide the basic

---

[12] Among those organisations whose anti-desertification activities DESCON and the IAWGD co-ordinate are: the Economic and Social Commission for Western Asia (ESCWA), the Economic and Social Commission for the Asia-Pacific Region (ESCAP), the Food and Agriculture Organisation of the UN (FAO), the United Nations Development Programme (UNDP), the International Atomic Energy Agency (IAEA), the United Nations Sudano-Sahelian Office (UNSO), the United Nations Educational, Scientific and Cultural Organisation (UNESCO), the World Meteorological Organisation (WMO), the Economic Commission for Africa (ECA), the Department of Technical Co-operation for Development (DTCD), the United Nations Industrial Development Organisation (UNIDO), the International Bank for Reconstruction and Development (IBRD) and the International Development Association (IDA) (Thomas & Middleton, 1994, pp.35-36).

framework and instrumentality which will guide the world community on an ongoing basis in its decisions on goals, targets, priorities, allocation of responsibilities and resources in respect of the many environment and development issues which will determine the future of our planet' (Johnson, 1993, p.25).

The World would be centrally planned by the philosopher-kings at the UN.

By the end of the fourth Preparatory Committee meeting, agreement had been reached on the 'Rio Declaration on Environment and Development'[13] and 85 per cent of Agenda 21 (Johnson, 1993, p.4). Then, in April 1992, a group of 'Eminent Persons' met in Tokyo to agree upon a Declaration on Financing Global Environment and Development, which, echoing Lord Dufferin, proclaimed:

'The human future is at risk. Wasteful patterns of production and consumption in industrialised countries, together with pervasive poverty and population growth in developing countries, are leading to the destruction of the Earth's ecological base and intolerable levels of human suffering and depravation. This dangerous course jeopardises the prospects for the survival and well-being of future generations.

'It is time to re-evaluate the thinking which underlies our present society. A new environmental ethic needs to be established, new value systems accepted and supported by the citizens at grass-roots levels ... adjusting our behaviour to the natural order that lies behind the limited and vulnerable ecosystems of the earth; and sharing environmental space equally among all countries of the Earth ...

[Therefore ...]

'Financing for sustainable development should not be viewed as 'foreign aid' in traditional terms; it is an essential investment in global environmental security' (Johnson, 1993, p.32).

Later in April 1992, officials from 55 developing countries met in Kuala Lumpur, to announce their own Declaration on Environment and Development, in which an implicit connection

---

[13] According to *The Earth Summit Bulletin* (16 June 1992), this is a list of '27 norms for state and interstate behaviour ... the declaration represents a very delicate balance of principles considered important by both developed and developing countries'.

between climate change, desertification and the need for resource transfers is made. The document notes:

'... the need for international efforts to address the serious problem of desertification and drought ... [w]e further stress that developed countries should make commitments for the provision of financial resources and transfer of technology to developing countries to enable them to adapt, mitigate and combat climate change and its adverse effects' (Johnson, 1993).

At UNCED, or 'The Earth Summit' as it is rather charmingly referred to, officials 'spoke of the need for $125 billion annually in transferred resources for implementing Agenda 21 (plus another $500 billion from the developing countries' own funds)' (Johnson, 1993, p.6).

Agenda 21 contains 40 chapters and runs to almost 600 pages. For the most part, the document treats desertification as synonymous with poverty and unsustainable development in arid, semi-arid and dry sub-humid regions (that is, much of the developing world). Over one-quarter of the proposed annual resource transfer of $125 billion was earmarked for 'sustainable agriculture and rural development', and was justified principally on the grounds that it would go towards 'poverty eradication' and stemming desertification.[14]

Agenda 21 does not commit signatories to indulge in such resource transfers, so officials set up the Global Environment Facility (GEF) – a conduit to transfer resources from 'wasteful' developed countries to developing countries stricken with 'pervasive poverty and population growth' – ostensibly, to limit the impact of 'global environmental problems'.[15] Officials from several African countries were reluctant to sign the conventions on Climate Change and Biodiversity, contending that desertification is a 'global problem' and that there should be commensurate GEF funding for 'anti-desertification' projects.[16]

---

[14] 'Promoting Sustainable Agriculture and Rural Development' alone is allocated $32·8 billion (*The Earth Summit*, pp.266-86).

[15] Climate change and biodiversity loss were promoted in the run-up to Rio as the principal 'global environmental problems'.

[16] Sustaining The Future Press Release: 'Legal Agreement to Curb Desertification to be Opened in Paris, 14-15 October,' Facsimile: United Nations Department of Public

These officials were placated by a proposal, '[t]o request the [UN] General Assembly ... to establish ... an *intergovernmental negotiating committee for the elaboration of an international convention to combat desertification* [INCD], in those countries experiencing serious drought and/or desertification, *particularly in Africa...*' (Johnson, 1993, p.244, emphasis added).

At its 47th session, the General Assembly of the UN duly passed resolution 47/188 establishing the INCD. In June 1994, at the INCD's fifth session, in Paris, a final negotiating text of the convention was agreed, and on 14-15 October 1994, in Paris, it was signed by officials from 87 nations (*The Network*, No. 41, Oct./Nov. 1994).[17]

The Convention on Desertification

The Convention on Desertification calls for the 'provision to affected developing countries, *particularly in Africa, of ... substantial financial resources*, including new and additional funding ...' Article 4 of the convention calls for parties to 'integrate strategies for *poverty eradication* into efforts to combat desertification and mitigate the effects of drought'; and to 'promote the use of existing *bilateral and multilateral financial mechanisms* and arrangements that mobilise and channel *substantial financial resources* to affected developing country parties in combating desertification and mitigating the effects of drought'. Article 3 of the regional implementation annex for Africa notes, 'the widespread poverty prevalent in most affected countries ... and their need for *significant amounts of external assistance*, in the form of grants and loans on concessional terms, *to pursue their development objectives*' (emphasis added).

Information, 10/10/94, p.3. Note that the Convention on Desertification contains the following passages: 'Bearing in mind the relationship between desertification and other environmental problems of global dimension facing the national and international communities ... Bearing also in mind the contribution that combating desertification can make in achieving the objectives of the United Nations Framework Convention on Climate Change, the Convention on Biological Diversity and other related conventions.'

[17] The convention will only come into force once 50 countries have ratified it (N. Oseiran, INCD secretariat, personal communication).

UNEP officials have called for $24 billion per year to be allocated to 'anti-desertification' projects over a 20-year period (EarthAction newsletter, October 1994). The following chapters question the wisdom of such spending.

2. Deserts, Dryland Degradation and the Myth of Desertification

According to the 1991 UNEP calendar:

'At least one third of the present global deserts are man-made, the result of millennia of human civilisation or, rather, the result of human misuse of the land.

'By the middle of the 20th century the problem had become global ... At present, desertification affects directly or marginally one quarter of the global land surface and almost one fifth of the world population.'

Such statements are highly emotive, conjuring up images of millions of people starving, their lands rapidly disappearing under a sea of sand. We are encouraged to recall pictures of malnourished and diseased African peasants, prostrate from exhaustion and heat exposure, helpless. This may well be the image officials at UNEP intended to convey. But it obscures the true nature of the problem of land degradation, leading to inaccurate assessments of its causes and inappropriate policies for its alleviation.

As Thomas and Middleton, authors of the UNEP World Atlas of Desertification, put it recently:

'The advancing desert concept may have been useful as a publicity tool but it is not one that represents the real nature of desertification processes' (Thomas & Middleton, 1994, pp.160-61).

This chapter begins with a brief description of the evolution of deserts. It then discusses the concepts of 'desertification' and desert encroachment and assesses the evidence for and against UNEP's claim that human misuse of the land is causing desertification.

Deserts and their Evolution

A desert can be uncontroversially defined as an 'uncultivated, sparsely inhabited tract of land' (*The New Shorter Oxford*

English Dictionary, 1993, p.644). But most deserts occur in arid areas (Cooke *et al.*, 1993)[1] where the soil is typically thin and often salty. Few plants have adapted to such environments and fewer still are palatable either to humans or to other mammals.

In order to assess the claim made by UNEP officials that one-third of today's deserts were caused by human misuse of land, we should first look at what causes the aridity which predisposed large tracts of land to becoming desert.

Cooke *et al.* (1993) identify five 'major climatic causes of aridity':

1. *Continentality*, that is, distance from marine or other moisture sources – because the dominant winds lose their moisture travelling over the continents.

2. *Dynamic anticyclonic subsidence* in the sub-tropics – this is part of the process by which the Earth's heat balance is maintained (through the global circulation of air currents) and is typically associated with warm winds and low relative humidity.

3. *Orographic influences*, namely air being forced downward in the lee of mountain ranges and being dried in the process.

4. *Upwelling* of cold water on some dry shore-lines, which encourages atmospheric stability and thereby reinforces aridity.

5. The *high albedo* (reflectivity) of the desert surface may reinforce aridity by increasing atmospheric stability.

---

[1] A useful measure of aridity is the ratio of mean annual precipitation (P) to the mean annual potential evapotranspiration rate (ETP). Using this measure, Cooke *et al.* define four zones of aridity:

(a) sub-humid zone $(0.50 < P/ETP < 0.75)$

(b) semi-arid zone $(0.20 < P/ETP < 0.50)$

(c) arid zone $(0.03 < P/ETP < 0.20)$

(d) hyper-arid zone $(0.03 > P/ETP)$

Most deserts occur in lands of type b, c or d.

The Sahara

While 'human misuse of the land' cannot be ruled out entirely as a cause of desert formation, little of the Sahara owes its existence to such factors. Indeed, the great tropical inland lakes of the Sahara began to dry out about 2·5 million years ago – over a million years before the ascent of man (Cooke *et al.*, 1993, p.424). Three main processes contributed to the aridification and desertification of the Sahara:

- Northwards movement of the African plate (since around 100 million years ago, when the Sahara was in the humid equatorial zone) (Cooke *et al.*, 1993, p.4).

- The uplifting of the Tibetan Plateau (approximately 40 million years ago)[2] caused a significant change in the global climatic system.[3]

- Climatic changes associated with the ice ages, the result most probably of periodic changes in the tilt of the earth's axis and its path around the sun. These have given periods of wetter and drier climate in the Sahara and other deserts (Andrew Warren, personal communication).

Since about 2·5 million years ago, the climate of the Sahara has been oscillating between long arid periods and brief bursts of greater humidity, with a cycle length of approximately 100,000 years. Shorter cycles of relative aridity and humidity have also occurred. Notably, at the peak of the last ice age, between 23,000 and 16,000 years ago, the Sahara was considerably more arid than it is today, extending about 450 km into the Sahel. Towards the end of the ice age, around 10,000 years ago, the Sahara was at the height of a more humid bout, with extensive lakes and swamps along the Blue and White Niles. Then, around 5,000

---

[2] This is known as the great Himalayan orogeny: during the course of the past 70 million years, the Tibetan plateau rose from below sea level to its present height – about 5 km above sea level.

[3] 'Continentality ... was greatly strengthened, the monsoon system became well established and north-western China became even more arid. Ancient lakes in the Tarim and other inland basins diminished ... and the Taklamakan and other sandy deserts probably enlarged considerably' (Cooke *et al.*, 1993, p.434).

years ago, the Sahara began to dry up again and has fluctuated about a mean state of hyper-aridity ever since (Cooke *et al.*, 1993). There is little evidence that the present extent of the Central Sahara was in any significant way altered by human misuse of land (see below).

Other Deserts

The evidence for human-induced desertification on a large scale in other areas is as scant and as highly contentious as it is for the Sahara, with climatic aridity, caused by similar processes to those operating in the Sahara, being a more credible explanation of the evolution of deserts.[4]

We may conclude that the world's deserts are primarily the product of geological and climatic changes beyond the control and influence of humans. While human misuse of land may have exacerbated aridification in certain places, these impacts were secondary and minor. The unsubstantiated claim made by UNEP officials that 'one-third of the present global deserts are man-made' therefore seems highly contentious.

'Desertification' Estimates

Another claim made by UNEP officials is that 'desertification affects ... almost one fifth of the world population. It is still progressing throughout the arid belt of the world, embracing new lands and new societies' (UNEP calendar, 1991). In particular, the Sahel region of Africa is, according to those same UNEP officials, 'the most stricken region of the world'.

Following USAID's unsubstantiated claim that the Sahara was expanding southward at a rate of about 30 miles per year (see above, Chapter 1), UNEP funded a study to estimate the true extent of desertification in the region. In this 1975 study, Hugh Lamprey surveyed the arid Saharan fringe of Northern Sudan from a light aircraft.[5] He then compared the desert boundary he

---

[4] Palaeomagnetic dating of loess deposits suggests that the Gobi and Ordos deserts are around 2 million years old and other deserts in Asia appear to be similarly ancient (Cooke *et al.*, 1993, pp.423-47).

[5] Lamprey made 10 North-South flights between 21 October and 10 November 1975 (Lamprey, 1988).

had seen from the plane with inferred vegetation records from 1958 and concluded that, 'It is evident that the desert's southern boundary has shifted south by an average of about 90-100 km in the last 17 years' (Lamprey, 1988).

UNEP subsequently commissioned the FAO, UNESCO and the WMO jointly to produce a map of 'desertification'. What was actually produced was a map of 'desertification hazard', that is, of the regions which *might* be affected in the way the lands on the desert margins of northern Sudan *appeared* to have been (Thomas & Middleton, 1994, p.50). Since there were no real data, the researchers simply made 'educated guesses' (Thomas & Middleton, 1994, p.51). Nevertheless, these guesses were subsequently presented at UNCOD, where delegates heard that:

> 'at least 35 per cent of the earth's land surface is now threatened by desertification, an area that represents places inhabited by 20 per cent of the world population. Each year 21 million hectares of once-productive soil are reduced by desertification to a level of zero or negative economic productivity, and six million hectares become total wasteland, beyond economic recoverability' (UNEP DC/PAC, 1990, p.1).

This assertion was made following submissions by 'a limited number of consultants with experience in drylands', whose estimates of the extent of 'at least moderate desertification' were aggregated to give a global figure of 3,970 million hectares.

In 1983 UNEP commissioned a new study to assess the extent of the 'desertification threat' as part of a general assessment of progress (GAP) on the impact of the PACD. This time a questionnaire was sent to government officials of 'afflicted' countries. Such a method of assessment is deeply flawed: *first*, since the level of anti-desertification tied foreign aid coming to a region is contingent on the reported level of desertification, there is a strong incentive to overstate the extent of desertification in that region;[6] *second*, since there had, in most cases, been no scientific assessment of the extent of the desertification threat (so there were almost no data), any claims made by these officials could not be refuted (a problem exacerbated by the

---

[6] This hypothesis is lent implicit support by the wide disparity between the Sudan's official estimates of desertification and the scientific evidence (see below, pp.36-38).

vagueness of UNEP's definition of desertification). Despite these incentives to overstate the extent of desertification, very few questionnaires were returned: even after UNEP sent consultants to 'help governments fill out the forms', the officials, 'found it difficult, if not impossible, to complete [them] correctly' (Thomas & Middleton, 1994, pp.52-53).

As a result, UNEP commissioned two more studies by its own experts to assess the global extent of the 'desertification threat'. The first of these, by Mabbutt, found that 2,001 million hectares of land were affected. The second, by Dregne, estimated the figure at 3,271 million hectares. The difference between these two figures was largely the result of differences in the definition of what constituted threatened land – Mabbutt had 'excluded large areas of what he considered to be remote, unwatered or otherwise difficult terrain, which although classified as rangeland was seldom if ever used as such' (Thomas & Middleton, 1994, p.55). However, the officials at UNEP were not happy with this divergence in opinion and asked Mabbutt to make a new assessment based more or less on Dregne's definition. Unsurprisingly, this new assessment, at 3,475 million hectares, was close to Dregne's.

In spite of this bureaucratic intervention, both of the 1984 GAP estimates of the area affected by desertification were lower than the 1977 estimate. Indeed, if we take Mabbutt's second estimate (the higher of the two) as the upper limit of the extent of desertification in 1984, then the total area of desertified land fell by 495 million hectares between 1977 and 1984 (about 70 million hectares per year). If the estimates of the extent of desertification made in 1977 and 1984 were credible, then the reduction in the area of threatened land might be taken to indicate that the UNEP antidesertification programme was working. Curiously, however, and in contradiction of the findings of GAP, UNEP continued to claim that the threat of desertification was becoming worse, causing 'approximately 21 million hectares annually to lose their productivity...' (Rozanov, 1990, p.49).

By the end of the 1980s, UNEP officials could no longer hide from the criticisms of their methodology for assessing the extent of the 'desertification threat,' especially since such criticisms were increasingly coming from within UNEP itself: in 1988, UNEP's Desertification Control Bulletin published a paper by Helldén which refuted Lamprey's conclusions (see below, p.37), and at least 'one scientist left the UNEP research programme in disgust at its poor research standards' (Pearce, 1992, p.42). In 1990 a UNEP official acknowledged that the map drawn up for UNCOD in 1977 'was based on geographical data which was [sic] not precise enough to assist future action in planning and guiding anti-desertification activities' (GAP II, 1990).

However, at the 1992 'Earth Summit' UNEP officials rekindled the desertification myth, stating that:

> 'Desertification affects about one sixth of the world's population, 70 per cent of all drylands, amounting to 3·6 billion hectares' (Pearce, 1992).

Defining Desertification

The term 'desertification' was first coined by André Aubréville (1949), who asserted that:

> 'ce sont des déserts qui naissent aujord'hui, sous nos yeux, dans de pays ou il tombe cependent annuellement de 700 a plus de 1,500 mm de pluies' ('deserts are being born today, in front of our eyes, in areas where the annual rainfall is between 700 and 1,500 mm').

Contrast this definition with that adopted by the UN at the recently signed Convention on Desertification: 'desertification is land degradation in arid, semi-arid and dry sub-humid areas resulting from various factors including climatic variations and human activities'. These divergent definitions are symptomatic of a literature which has become more interested in semantics than science.[7] That said, a reasoned debate about the existence of desertification, its causes and its consequences, clearly requires an adequate definition.

In UNEP's analyses, the presence or absence of particular kinds of soil and/or vegetation were used to infer the existence of a 'desertification threat'. However, western 'experts' disagree

---

[7] For an overview of definitions of desertification see: Odingo (1990); Glantz and Orlovsky (1984); Helldén (1991).

both amongst themselves and, more especially, with indigenous people about what these indicators truly signify. For example, soil stoniness is typically viewed by western 'experts' as an indicator of erosion, the result of 'over-cultivation', but to Ethiopian peasants stones indicate that the soil is becoming 'stronger'. Recent evidence suggests that the indigenous people are correct (Darling, 1993, p.2).

In addition, a change in the type of vegetation in an area is often just a change, and not, as many desertification 'experts' claim, a sign of imminent desertification. For example, Patrick Darling found that in one drought-ridden place in Mali, cattle had denuded the area of the grasses on which they grazed. In response, the peasants switched to herding goats, which could survive by eating acacia from the surrounding area. The goats then excreted acacia seeds onto the recently denuded land. When the rains returned, the denuded grassland was replaced with acacia, enabling the peasants to increase their herds of goats (Patrick Darling, personal communication).

This failure to measure 'desertification' objectively using only evidence from soil composition and/or vegetation, has led some experts to suggest alternative measures. These typically include some measure of the economic value of the output of land. In a report prepared for the UNCED, Warren and Khogali (1990, p.6) propose the following 'three environmental predicaments' faced by the Sudano-Sahelian region as a 'further refinement of ... the concept' of desertification:

- '*Drought* is a period of two years or more with rainfall well below average...

- '*Desiccation* is a process of aridification resulting from a dry period lasting on the order of decades...

- '*Dryland degradation* is land degradation in drylands brought about mainly by inappropriate land use under delicate environmental conditions. Land degradation is a persistent decrease in the productivity of vegetation and soils' (Warren & Khogali, 1990).

Mortimore (1990, p.200) suggests that such 'chains of cause and effect ... are easier to hypothesise than to demonstrate', offering instead a more catholic definition:

- Desertification is 'the degradation of ecosystems in arid or semi-arid regions, where "degradation" means the loss of primary productivity' (Mortimore, 1990, p.18).

Mortimore's definition, adopted here, has the advantage of being more readily testable, since '[l]osses in productivity, irrespective of the past or future state of the ecosystem, can be measured objectively over time' (Mortimore, 1990, p.18). Once desertification has been established, 'objective' comparison can be made between the condition of land used by humans with land not so used, thereby providing evidence for or against human causation.

Evidence of Desertification and Desert Encroachment

We now turn to empirical analyses which attempt to measure the extent of desertification and desert encroachment. These analyses fall into three categories: macroscopic studies, which attempt to plot the changing boundaries of desert systems (and hence the extent of any desert encroachment); microscopic studies, which attempt to measure the changes in productivity of specific ecosystems (that is, the extent of desertification); and integrated studies which test for both desertification (using microscopic data) and desert encroachment (using macroscopic data).

The first group of such studies is concerned with evaluating the claims made by USAID, UNEP and others[8] that the southern boundary of the Sahara has been expanding.

Integrated Studies of the Sudan

In a paper in UNEP's Desertification Control Bulletin, Suliman quotes a 1988 report by the Sudanese government in which the following claim is made:

---

[8] Robert McNamara, whilst President of the World Bank, is reported to have argued that 'We must now stop the advance of the desert ... in Mali the Sahara has been drawn 350 kilometres south by desertification over the past 20 years' (quoted by Forse, 1989).

'It has been estimated that 650,000 square kilometres of the Sudan had been desertified over the last 50 years and that the front-line has been advancing at a rate of 90-100 kilometres annually during the last 19 years' (Suliman, 1988).[9]

Since the late 1970s a group of scientists at the University of Lund in Sweden have been carrying out integrated studies of the Sudan using advanced remote-sensing techniques, extensive field observations, national statistics (crops, population, precipitation) and spatial monitoring to assess the density of vegetation and the causes of changes in the productivity of land at the southern boundary of the Sahara in the Sudan. In support of this methodology, Helldén (1991, p.377) notes that 'For national and regional monitoring there are no practical alternatives to the use of repeated satellite observations'.

In 1984 Helldén published a paper describing the results of these studies. A shortened version of this paper was published in UNEP's *Desertification Control Bulletin* in 1988, which concluded that:

'There was no creation of long lasting desert-like conditions during the 1962-1979 period in the area corresponding to the magnitude described by many authors. There was however a severe drought impact on crop yield during the Sahelian drought 1964-1974. The drought effects on the natural vegetation productivity was probably of the same magnitude. The impact of the Sahelian drought was short lasting followed by a fast land productivity recovery' (Helldén, 1988).

Thus, in Helldén's opinion, and based upon the most rigorous integrated studies carried out in the Sudan, there is no evidence of either desert encroachment or human-induced desertification. Whilst there was indeed some temporary desertification, this was most probably the result of drought and was reversed once the rains returned.

A follow-up study carried out by the Lund group, 'prolonging the high resolution digital satellite data ... time series with 1990

---

[9] This may be a misinterpretation of Lamprey's study for UNEP, in which he concluded that 'the desert's southern boundary has shifted south by an average of about 90-100 km in the last 17 years' (Lamprey, 1988), which works out at approximately 5-6 km annually.

and 1991 imagery and recent field surveys and national statistics on agriculture and precipitation ... so far confirm the results indicated above' (Helldén, 1991, p.379).

Macroscopic Studies of the Sahel Region

H. E. Dregne, one of UNEP's desertification experts,[10] and C. J. Tucker have analysed satellite images representing the normalised difference vegetation index (NDVI) which shows how the density of vegetative cover at the Southern boundary of the Sahara changes over time.[11] In a paper published in the same issue of UNEP's *Desertification Control Bulletin* in which Suliman quoted the Sudanese government statistics, Dregne and Tucker (1988) showed that any desert encroachment in the Sahel had been strictly temporary. And, in concordance with Helldén, they saw drought as the primary cause of this temporary desertification.

In addition, Dregne and Tucker (1988) show that temporary drought-induced desert encroachment occurs more generally along the entire southern boundary of the Sahara (although 'regional differences [in extent] are marked'). Moreover, they point out that even if there was

'a permanent vegetational shift of 5 to 6 km per year [we] would require perhaps 30 to 40 years of observation by meteorological satellites and ground studies before it would be possible to conclude that the shift was indeed permanent'.

In any case, they continue,

'[a] permanent shift of 5 km per year seems to be rather fast ... [While,] if the desertification were patchy, as it usually is, the time for determining whether changes were temporary or permanent probably would be even longer'.

Dregne and Tucker (1988) conclude with an emphatic rejection of the 'encroaching Sahara' theory: 'Attractive though

---

[10] Dregne produced one of the two 'expert' assessments of the extent of the global desertification threat for UNEP's 1984 GAP. He now runs the International Centre for Arid and Semi-Arid Land Studies (ICASALS), which produced GAP II in 1992.

[11] The NDVI data came from the Advanced Very High Resolution Radiometer carried on polar-orbiting meteorological satellites of the US National Oceanic and Atmospheric Administration.

the "encroaching Sahara" idea is, it is no more credible now than it was in Stebbing's day.'

A follow-up study, carried out by Tucker *et al.* (1991) using NDVI data over the period 1980-1990, has confirmed the existence of these dramatic interannual and interseasonal shifts in the vegetative boundary of the Sahel/Sahara.

Microscopic Studies

Microscopic studies consider the long-term changes in productivity of land around settlements on the edge of the Sahara as a result of changes in climate, population and adaptive land use patterns. Such a study has been carried out by Michael Mortimore (1990), who analysed the impact of the prolonged drought of the 1970s and 1980s on crop production in Kano state, Northern Nigeria (an area Mortimore had known personally since the late 1960s). Using photographs from 1950 and 1969, combined with a field study carried out in 1986, he analysed changes in the extent of bare dunes around a sample of five Kano villages and found that the total area of moving sand in village perimeter dunes declined from 194 hectares in 1950 to 160 hectares in 1986.

While Mortimore (1990) found that bare dunes in rangeland areas, non-existent in 1950, accounted for around 20 per cent of the rangeland in 1986, he noted that the Anglo-French Forestry Commission observed similar live dunes in 1937, which suggested that they were an intermittent feature of the rangeland, probably caused in large part by drought stress.[12] In addition, he notes that the same Forestry Commission 'reported the boundaries of the Manga Grasslands at three locations (west, east and south), and they are found in exactly the same places today' (Mortimore, 1990, p.185).

Although deforestation had resulted in the replacement of woodlands with grasslands in many places over the period

---

[12] Mortimore (1990, p.184) explained the increase in incidence of rangeland dunes as follows:

'[W]e may tentatively conclude that rangeland dunes began to develop under grazing pressure, but their growth in size and numbers accelerated, after 1969, under conditions of drought stress.'

(1950-1986), the 'existence of any linkage [of this change] with the reactivation of moving dunes is unproven' (Mortimore, 1990, p.164). Moreover, '[r]ainfall variations ... are primarily responsible for changes in the condition of the grass, both from year to year and in the longer term. ... But the capacity of annual grasses to regenerate vigorously after intensive grazing and poor rainfall has been demonstrated beyond doubt' (Mortimore, 1990, pp.167-68).

For the final word on whether the temporary desertification of the rangeland should be attributed to human misuse of land or to climatic influences, Mortimore (1990, p. 186) deferred to indigenous wisdom: 'Any farmer or stockowner in the grasslands would call the problem under-precipitation, not over-exploitation.'

Tiffen, Mortimore and Gichuki (1994) have carried out the most detailed microscopic study of environmental change in drylands. Taking the Machakos district of Kenya as a case study, the authors explore 'the relationship between increasing population density, productivity and environmental degradation ... over the period 1930-1990' (Tiffen *et al.*, 1994, p.13). Taking such a long term perspective, in a district which has had, '[i]n less than a century of recorded rainfall in the two rainy seasons of each year ... 90 droughts' (Tiffen *et al.*, 1994, p.5), enabled the authors more readily to test the hypothesis that desertification was a transient and cyclical phenomenon induced by bouts of aridity.

Chapter 3 discusses some of Tiffen *et al.*'s conclusions in more detail, but in the context of the above hypothesis they note that '[t]he rainfall record ... suggests a strong link between periods of drought, denudation of grazing lands, and intensified erosion' (pp.117-18). In addition, the period 1930 to 1990 saw an approximately threefold increase in the value of output *per capita*, and a tenfold increase in the value of output per hectare, whilst the population density rose fivefold (Tiffen *et al.*, 1994, p.13). Thus, we can conclude that desertification has not been a significant problem in Machakos District. Indeed, as Tiffen *et al.* (1994, p.200) point out, '[t]he degradation problem feared in the 1930s has been reversed'.

Indigenous Perceptions

Researchers working for SOS Sahel, a pressure group which calls for more resources to be transferred to the Sahel region, have carried out interviews with tribal people the length and breadth of the Sahel.[13] Whilst many of the reported interviews with younger people indicate concern that land degradation had worsened during their lifetime, some of those whose memories stretch further back suggested that such concern was unwarranted. For example, Godauna Halake, a 96-year-old woman from Kafate in the Borena province of Ethiopia, noted that:

> 'During drought, the landscape goes dry. However, when it rains again, there is enough grass. I have not seen any big change in the rainfall pattern over my life' (Cross and Barker, 1992, p.219).

Conclusions

This chapter has attempted to redress the balance of the debate begun when officials at UNEP claimed that human misuse of land had caused at least one-third of the world's deserts and was resulting in a rapid expansion of those deserts. Given the historical evolution of the world's deserts, it seems unlikely that many were caused primarily by human action. Macroscopic analyses of land use in arid regions suggest that desert encroachment is largely mythical, while microscopic studies suggest that the principal cause of (temporary) desertification has been drought stress.

However, the existence of land degradation (particularly soil erosion and salinisation) in much of Africa (not just in arid areas) is testimony to the inappropriateness of certain types of land use. Chapters 4 and 5 offer an explanation of these phenomena.

---

[13] SOS Sahel receives approximately 60 per cent of its funding from governments (SOS Sahel Annual Report, 1993). This particular project was funded by: NORAD, the EC, HelpAge, the International Institute for Environment and Development, the Linnean Society and Womankind. Funding for publication came from: NOVIB, HelpAge, Christian Aid, Ernest Kleinwort Charitable Trust, Thomas Sivewright Catto Charitable Settlement and the UN Trust for Ageing.

3. Dismal Predictions: Climate Change and Population Pressure

Chapter 2 considered the claim that human action has been a primary cause of desertification in the past. In this chapter we consider the claim that land degradation is likely to occur in the future as a result of human-induced climate change and/or population pressure. As one World Bank paper put it:

'Our own hypothesis would be that about 70 per cent of the [desertification] problem can be attributed to natural events [including climate change] and population growth...' (Nelson, 1990).

Human-Induced Changes in the Composition of the Earth's Atmosphere

Since the mid-19th century, humans have been gradually extracting large quantities of decayed organic matter (coal, oil, and natural gas). At the same time, commercial production of live biomass (especially rice and cows) and extraction of minerals (for instance, sulphur and chlorine salts) have increased dramatically. Much of the decayed organic matter has been burnt (oxidised) to form carbon monoxide, carbon dioxide and water, whilst simultaneously releasing a multitude of other organic and inorganic compounds. One frequent side reaction of this process is the oxidisation of atmospheric nitrogen, giving dinitrogen oxide, nitrous oxide and nitrogen dioxide. In addition, the oxidisation of coal typically results in the release of sulphur dioxide.

Using both organic and inorganic matter, humans have synthesised a large number of chemicals. Among these are the chloroflurocarbons (CFCs). Live biomass, in particular rice paddies and cows, as well as decaying dead biomass, produce methane. Carbon dioxide, nitrogen oxides, CFCs and methane have all been identified as 'greenhouse gases' (GHGs). GHGs cause the atmosphere to warm because they are relatively transparent to the long wavelength electromagnetic radiation emitted by the Sun but relatively opaque to the short wavelength electromagnetic radiation emitted by the Earth (IPCC, 1990, 1992).

The increase in concentration of the GHGs, as a result of the human activities mentioned above, has led to speculation that the Earth's atmosphere might be becoming warmer.[1] However, the relationship between GHG concentration and atmospheric temperature is known to be non-linear. Incomplete understanding both of the waveband saturation effect and of the multitude of complex climatic feedback effects has meant that the relationship between GHG concentration and global climatic change remains poorly understood. Add to this the fact that much of the temperature data collected over the past century has been biassed by poor measurement techniques, and it is evident that predictions of future climatic change are mere speculation.[2]

There is a consensus amongst atmospheric scientists that any climatic change induced by increased concentrations of GHGs will not occur simply as a general 'global warming'. The most likely effect is a reduction in the diurnal temperature differential, as night-time temperatures rise and daytime temperatures remain largely unchanged. In addition, these changes are expected to occur more in polar regions than in the tropics (IPCC, 1990, 1992).

The Impact of CO_2

There is insufficient space here for a full discussion of the intricacies of the climate change debate. However, it is worth considering the impact of an increase in the concentration of carbon dioxide (CO_2). Many have claimed that CO_2 is the most damaging of all GHGs.[3] However, recent research contradicts this claim.

---

[1] The contrast between the 1990s and the 1970s is striking: during this earlier era of environmental consciousness, the main concern seems to have been that the Earth was becoming cooler. Lamb (1974), for example, expected global cooling to result in horrific droughts in the Sahel as the P/ETP rate declined.

[2] The speculation has been adumbrated by IPCC (1990, 1992); on the waveband saturation effect see Bottcher (1992) and Barrett (1995); on the data problem see Balling (1992); for a general overview see Michaels (1992) and Bate and Morris (1994).

[3] See, for example, the Policymakers Summary of the IPCC reports (IPCC, 1990, 1992).

CO_2 absorbs radiation in two fairly narrow bands of the electromagnetic spectrum. Once all the radiation in these wavebands emitted by the Earth is absorbed by CO_2 already present, increasing the CO_2 concentration would have no warming effect. This is known as the 'saturation effect'. Barrett (forthcoming) has argued that since CO_2 concentration is currently close to saturation level (it is estimated that about 85 per cent of CO_2-absorbing wavebands are saturated), increases in CO_2 concentration are unlikely to have a significant impact on atmospheric temperature.

Plants require CO_2 to survive – combining water with CO_2 in the presence of sunlight, through photosynthesis, they create cellulose, the basic building block of all plants. It follows, and has been shown empirically, that increasing the concentration of atmospheric CO_2 results in an increase in the rate of growth of most plants. In many cases this effect continues to CO_2 concentrations three or more times current levels. In addition, increasing the atmospheric concentration of CO_2 reduces the concentration of water required for plant growth (because plants produce more leaf stomata) (Idso, 1991).

Taking the above effects together, we would expect that a large increase in the atmospheric concentration of CO_2 would lead to a small reduction in the diurnal temperature differential and a large increase in the rate of growth of most crops.

This would seem to be good news for farmers in the arid parts of the world: output per hectare would be increased at no extra cost to the farmer, and droughts would be less damaging, since the water requirements of crops would be lower and the reduction in albedo effect of the land (as a result of increased vegetative cover) is likely to lower surface temperatures and may induce increased precipitation (Balling, 1991).[4]

Premature Predictions from the Population Prophets

In the second century AD, Tertullian, a Carthaginian priest, claimed that:

---

[4] If temperatures do rise, then global average P/ETP is also expected to rise, although there is considerable uncertainty over the distributional impact of P/ETP changes (Schneider *et al.*, 1990).

'Our numbers are burdensome to the World, which can hardly support us ... In very deed, pestilence, and famine, and wars, and earthquakes have been regarded as a remedy for nations, as the means of pruning the luxuriance of the human race' (cited by Kasun, 1988, p.46).

For the past 1,800 years population pessimists, from Saint Jerome to Thomas Malthus, have invoked similar arguments.

In his 'Essay Concerning the Principle of Population', Malthus asserted 'that the power of population is indefinitely greater than the power in the earth to produce sustenance for man' (Malthus, 1976, p.20). This assertion rests on the assumption that any increase in the wellbeing of a peasant, brought about by an increase in productivity, will simply induce that peasant to have more children and thereby return to the level of subsistence. But why, one might well ask, would a peasant who has laboured hard to improve his lot spend all his surplus on having more children? As Schumpeter notes, 'the old idea ... that the production of foodstuffs ... creates its own demand because people will multiply as it expands,' is 'as persistent as it [is] useless' (Schumpeter, 1954, p.191).

Choosing the Size of the Family

Most arguments supporting population control policies assume either (1) that individuals are not making choices about the number of children they have, but are merely following 'custom', or (2) that although mothers choose to have fewer children, they lack the means to reduce the number of pregnancies.

Taking the second argument first: most authors equate reduction in pregnancies with the use of some contraceptive device (an IUD, a condom, a diaphragm, spermicidal jelly, 'the pill', etc.). However, surveys carried out in Pakistan in 1990/91 and in Bulgaria in 1977 found that only about 10 per cent of couples in either nation were using contraceptive devices, but while women in Pakistan gave birth to an average of six children over their life, women in Bulgaria gave birth to an average of only 2·2 (Eberstadt, 1995, p.20). This difference is explained by Harvard economist Nicholas Eberstadt as follows:

'The reason fertility levels can differ by a factor of three when levels of usage for modern contraceptive methods are virtually identical is that parental preferences rather than medical technology are the decisive factor in determining a society's average family size' (Eberstadt, 1995, p. 20).

As to the claim that women are not making choices about the number of children they have, a recent study for the World Bank estimated that at least 90 per cent of the variations in fertility levels between developing countries can be explained by differences in the desired levels of fertility reported by local women (Pritchett & Summers, 1994). Those who believe that these are not individual choices but the programmed responses of women indoctrinated by an oppressive culture might do well to consider the possibility that their own attitudes are less than culturally objective.

Population Growth, Poverty and Environmental Degradation

At the recent UN Conference on Population and Development, officials repeatedly claimed that population growth is a very significant deterrent to development. However, the evidence from most developing countries suggests that this is not so.[5] Although there may occasionally be a correlation between population growth and a decline in *per capita* income (to take one arbitrary measure of the apparent cost of extra people), this does not show that the growth in population has of itself caused the decline.[6] One of the most forceful arguments made by the proponents of population control is that even when individuals choose how many children they have, they may have 'too many'

---

[5] Whilst it is true that raising children is costly, it is also true that once those children are able to help out on the land, they may provide a crucial extra pair of hands, enabling the family to build a stone terrace, to reduce soil erosion; or to plant a row of trees, which provide shade for the plants below and fuel from the wood. Add to this the possibility that those children might one day invent a new technology which enables the production of more food on less land and it becomes far from clear that 'the hands do not produce as much' (Malthus, 1976, p.26).

[6] On this topic see, for example, Eberstadt (1994), who notes that 'It is an elementary lapse in logic – a fallacy in composition – to conclude that poverty is a 'population problem' simply because it is manifest in populations' (p.6).

46

children because they do not carry all the costs of having those children.[7]

In practice, of course, it is impossible for anyone but the individuals affected to measure either the costs or the benefits of having a baby, since these things are entirely subjective (hence, if more than one person is affected the aggregate benefits or costs cannot be known). However, it is instructive to discuss one example from Africa where the 'Population Principle' has not resulted in environmental degradation – quite the opposite in fact. In this case, the externalities from having children seem to have been positive, that is, instead of imposing a net cost on society each child creates a net benefit.

Machakos: More People, Less Erosion

Tiffen *et al.* (1994) carried out a longitudinal study of the Machakos district of Kenya, showing how the people of the Akamba tribe adapted to changing circumstances in a number of ways.

At the end of the 19th century, population densities in Machakos were low because many people had died during a long and severe drought. The abundance of fertile land led people to have many children – children were considered desirable because they could help out on the family farm, making life for their parents easier and providing for them in their old age. As the population grew, people cleared new land for cultivation. However, the area of uninhabited land diminished, giving rise to three adaptations:

- *first*, some people migrated for part of the year to work in nearby towns;

- *second*, some people invested in more intensive agriculture – building terraces, planting trees, growing more valuable crops (such as coffee);

---

[7] This might occur, for example, where the state provides certain goods (housing, medical care, food stamps), or where the state prevents private ownership of certain goods (such as land). This is an example of the tragedy of the collective (see Chapter 5, below, p.68).

- *third*, some people became traders – buying and selling goods.

Through these adaptations, the population density of Machakos district and the *per capita* income of the inhabitants of Machakos grew simultaneously (see above, Chapter 2, especially p.40).

In addition, over the same period the condition of the soil in Machakos has improved enormously: in 1930 much of the district suffered from severe soil erosion, but by 1990 this had largely stopped, with regrowth evident in many of the eroded gullies and a reduction in the amount of sheet erosion. Moreover, the Akamba are now better able to cope with drought: in 1984, at the height of the most severe drought this century, *per capita* output was twice that during the 1960/61 drought.

These observations can be explained as follows. Most indigenous farmers in Africa, including the Akamba, rely on members of their extended family to provide labour for producing crops and grazing animals. However, few families are self sufficient in all desired commodities. Instead, they produce surpluses of some goods and then exchange these for other goods they need or desire. As the population density of an area increases, each family need produce less of its own food requirements, since these can be obtained more and more through exchange with other families. So, families will tend to specialise in the production of certain commodities. Specialisation enables farmers to experiment with new or innovative technologies – different types and combinations of crops, different methods of soil conservation, fodder for cattle, and so on.

Over time, this experimentation is likely to lead to more efficient farming practices – farmers learn which crops are better suited to their land, so they are able to produce more food per acre and per capita. The larger surpluses are then exchanged for different foods, other goods (such as cooking utensils and clothes) and services (such as credit) produced by other families who have also specialised. In this way, everybody benefits from the rise in population and the growth of the market.

So long as these indigenous people continue to be driven by a desire to improve their lot, and are not inhibited from doing so by intervention in their business (see Chapter 5), they are likely to continue to innovate and adopt more efficient technologies for producing food, goods and services.

This example shows that sustainable development[8] can be the outcome of individuals spontaneously adapting to changing circumstances.[9] In addition, it shows that sustainable development can go hand in hand with population growth. Moreover, it negates the claim, made in the Brundtland Report[10], in Agenda 21, and in the Convention on Desertification, that poverty itself causes environmental degradation.[11] Machakos is not an isolated example:[12] Eberstadt states that, 'despite rapid world population growth, global improvements in per capita output levels have been unprecedented in the twentieth century, and show no sign as yet of stopping' (Eberstadt, 1994).[13]

Conclusions

In this chapter, it has been argued that neither climate change nor population expansion is causing desertification. Whilst the

---

[8] As Eberstadt (1995, p.43) puts it: 'the entire purpose of modern economic development...is...extension of human choice.' In which case, the purpose of sustainable (economic) development is the continuous extension of human choice.

[9] In Machakos, some technologies were either introduced or imposed by officials of the administration. It is unclear, however, whether the introduction of beneficial technologies (for example, terracing) outweighed the imposition of detrimental ones (such as destocking). See below, Chapter 5, for a discussion of this topic.

[10] This was the 1987 report of the World Commission on Environment and Development. Also known as *Our Common Future*, the report was nicknamed the *Brundtland Report* after the chairperson of the Commission, Gro Brundtland, then Prime Minister of Norway.

[11] The Brundtland Report proclaims that 'Poverty itself pollutes the environment'. Agenda 21 proclaims that 'A specific anti-poverty strategy is therefore one of the basic conditions for ensuring sustainable development'. The Convention on Desertification proclaims that 'poverty eradication ... [is] essential to meeting sustainability objectives'.

[12] For a discussion of adaptation to peculiar environments amongst indigenous people in pre-colonial times, see Schneider (1986).

[13] Of course, past trends may not continue into the future and Eberstadt is careful to point out that the relationship between population growth and economic growth is extremely complex. It may or may not be the case, for example, that an extra pair of hands will on average provide social benefits – because they seem to have done so up to now does not imply that they will always do so.

impacts of changes in the atmospheric concentration of trace gases, and of changes in the density of human population, are contingent on a number of other factors, some tentative forecasts might be offered:

- An increase in carbon dioxide is likely to result in both an increase in agricultural productivity in arid regions and an increase in precipitation, so famines will be fewer and less severe.

- An increase in population, in the absence of coercive intervention, is likely to result in an increase in *per capita* income, as entrepreneurs, motivated by a desire to better their lot, innovate and adapt technologies and institutions to changing circumstances.

PART II

The Political Economy of Land Degradation

4. The Political Economy of Africa

This chapter presents a very brief overview of the evolution of the socio-political environment in developing countries. It is intended as a precursor to the discussion, in chapter five, of the root causes of land degradation – and the myths surrounding it – and, in chapter six, of some tentative proposals for policy reform.

For the most part, these matters are discussed in relation to Africa because so much of the development debate, and most of UNEP's anti-desertification programme, have been concentrated on Africa.[1]

Indigenous African Institutions

Prior to the 'scramble for Africa' by Europeans (which occurred between 1876 and 1912, according to Pakenham, 1991, p.xxvii), the continent was inhabited by hundreds of diverse tribes, each of which had its own customs and institutions. Many tribes had rudimentary, but highly democratic, political institutions. The hierarchy of these polities was roughly as follows: first was the chief (or, in some instances, king), who provided the link between the tribe and its ancestors, and was authorised to resolve disputes between members of the tribe; second was the privy council, which advised the chief on all matters relating to the tribe; third was the council of elders, which was made up from the oldest members of each lineage within the tribe and advised the chief on more serious matters; finally, there was the village assembly, where each member of the tribe could have a say (Ayittey, 1991, pp.71-149).

---

[1] This concentration of attention on Africa has continued despite the fact that UNEP's own estimates indicate that the threat from desertification is greatest in Asia: according to the UN's *EarthAction* newsletter (October 1994), 'Asia loses $21 billion per year, Africa $9 billion, Australia $3 billion, Europe $1 billion, North America $5 billion and South America $3 billion' from desertification. The most plausible explanation for this is that famine in Africa, and not desertification itself, tends to be the great mobiliser of funds because starvation produces more sympathy than soil erosion.

However, a number of tribes had no chief or privy council to provide central authority. They were stateless societies, but they appeared to exhibit relatively few of the problems claimed to be inherent in such anarchies – there was no 'warre ... of every man, against every man', nor was life, 'solitary, poore, nasty, brutish, and short', as Hobbes (1991, p.88-89) had warned.[2] Bates (1984) explains the stability of one of these societies, the Nuer of Sudan, in the framework of a repeated game: potential problems (such as theft of cattle) were prevented because rational self-seeking individuals realise that the costs of stealing from someone with whom one repeatedly interacts are greater than the benefits (see also: Axelrod, 1984, Sugden, 1986, Ostrom, 1988, 1990, and Ellickson, 1991).

Tribes without a central authority relied on entrepreneurs and voluntary associations to provide public goods such as the markets where goods were traded.[3] However, even in tribes with a chief, many of these public goods were provided voluntarily: for example, among the Guru of the Ivory coast, 'the founder of a market was usually a pre-eminent and rich individual, a *fua*, who sought social recognition' (Meissalloux, 1962).

Bates found that, of the tribes he analysed, those with more centralised political systems tended to have higher population densities, a more evolved market structure, and carried out more trade with outsiders; he offers the following explanation of the evolution of centralisation:

'Those who seek power seek private advantages; they, like the rest of us, seek more of the good things of life, and they turn to the exercise of power to gain them. But, to win and retain political power, political aspirants must attract followers, and to do so they must offer advantages, such as the opportunity to prosper. To secure

[2] Nor was there a 'oneness with nature', as Rousseau seemed to think existed in the state of nature. Rather, there was a system of evolved customs which limited the number of intra-tribal disputes.

[3] Samuelson (1954) defined a public good as a product 'which all enjoy in common in the sense that each individual's consumption of that good leads to no subtraction from any other individual's consumption of that good.' A market is a public good in this sense, since all those who trade in the market benefit from its existence – each exchange benefits both parties to the exchange, so that no individual's consumption of the market is subtracting from any other individual's consumption of it. See also: Cowen (1992), and Foldvary (1994).

disproportionate benefits, they must generate benefits which can be shared' (Bates, 1984, p.41).

The chief of an African tribe conferred two obvious benefits upon the members of that tribe:

- *First*, he offered a cheap mechanism for resolving disputes over land use. As population density rose, land became more scarce and conflicts over its use occurred more frequently, so a cheap method of dispute resolution was probably seen as desirable – especially to those who believed they would benefit from the distribution of land that would result if it was chosen by the chief they supported (Ault and Rutman, 1979).

- *Second*, he could ensure the security of outside traders. While repeated interaction prevents transgression of tribal norms against fellow members of a tribe, it does not necessarily prevent a member of one tribe stealing from a member of another tribe. But the chief of a tribe can prevent such transgressions by threatening the use of force (removal of usufruct, etc.). So, a trader from another tribe wishing to travel in safety would be willing to pay the chief a 'dash'[4] as a means of securing his coercive authority.

Exit and Voice – Checks on the Coercive Power of the Chief

Clearly, the provision of security by a coercive monopolist benefited those engaging in trade with outsiders. To the extent that this trade also enriched the whole tribe (for instance, through secondary trading and gifts), the provision of security was a public good. Whether the provision of such public goods in this manner is worth the loss of freedom entailed in the coercion required to produce them is a subjective matter.

In any case, members of African tribes were usually free to leave their tribe and join or form another tribe – they had the right of exit – and, through the village assembly, they could object to the dictates of the chief – they had the right of voice.

---

[4] Ayittey (1991, p.122-24), notes that a 'dash' is more of a payment in advance for some service the chief has contracted to provide, rather than a bribe.

These two rights reinforced one another, providing a constant check to excessive coercion by the chief.[5]

Rent Seeking

In the above example, outside traders paid the chief a dash in return for security. But it is probable that members of the tribe who wanted to trade with outsiders also lobbied or bribed the chief into providing security through coercion. Such lobbying (or bribery) can be termed 'political entrepreneurship', since entrepreneurial gains are obtained through the provision of a good by a central body with a monopoly of power (a *polis*, or state).[6]

Tullock (1967) has provided a theoretical model in which to view the costs of suborning (bribing or lobbying) state officials (kings, chiefs, politicians, and civil servants): a central authority with a monopoly of power can choose to provide a monopoly of other services. So, the existence of such a central authority provides an incentive for political entrepreneurs to suborn state officials for the provision of services they demand, be it security, schools, or space rockets. As the number of services supplied by the state increases, the potential for welfare losses from subornation increases, as more and more special interests attempt to get a slice of the cake.

In addition, because the choice of the monopoly provider of a service is made by state officials, there is a constant incentive for political entrepreneurs to suborn state officials to award the

---

[5] Ayittey (1991) provides several examples of tribes who 'destooled' their chief for engaging in corrupt behaviour – an eloquent example of the power of voice, while the sheer multiplicity of African tribes is testimony to the power of exit. See also Hirschman (1970).

[6] To calculate the social efficiency of this outcome, the cost of lobbying (or bribing) the chief and the loss of autonomy resulting from the centralisation of authority would have to be weighed against the reduction in transaction costs *vis-à-vis* voluntary provision. Given the subjective nature of the costs associated with the loss of autonomy and the difficulty of measuring the transaction costs of either types of provision, it is not possible to say whether centralisation represents a 'welfare loss' or a 'welfare gain'. However, the fact that members of stateless tribes often voluntarily chose to obey the will of an outside chief, who ensured the security of traders, suggests that the transaction costs of achieving such voluntary provision were not an insurmountable barrier, and may have been a worthwhile price to pay for the maintenance of autonomy.

contract to them, so they may gain the monopoly rents available. This subornation represents a welfare loss. Moreover, when a central authority holds a monopoly of power, that central authority can create legislation which favours the interests of political entrepreneurs. For example, inefficient industries might suborn state officials to protect them from foreign competition by imposing trade barriers.[7] Anne Krueger has termed the behaviour of such political entrepreneurs 'rent-seeking', since they seek out the rents available through abuse of the state's coercive monopoly of power.[8]

As the behaviour of tribal chiefs suggests, politicians, like other people, act principally in a self-interested manner (Smith, 1776; Buchanan and Tullock, 1962).[9] In the case of a democracy, this self-interested behaviour probably manifests itself primarily in the desire to become re-elected (Tullock, 1993). So politicians in a democracy will, on the whole, favour those rules which increase their chances of becoming re-elected. In an autocracy, however, the rules are set so as to increase allegiance to the autocrat (Zolberg, 1966; Nettl and Robertson, 1968; Gellar, 1973; Jackson and Rosberg, 1982; Tullock, 1987; Sawyer, 1988).

Redistribution and 'Aid'

Tullock (1975) shows how redistributive policies elicit perverse responses from potential recipients. Self-seeking individuals will indulge in self-neglect, and even self-mutilation, in an attempt to win aid from the state. For example, if the rules of the polity state that a person with a broken leg must be given medical care, but paupers will otherwise be left to fend for themselves, then it

---

[7] By raising the cost of imported goods, such barriers make the (otherwise more expensive) goods produced by indigenous manufacturers appear cheaper to domestic customers.

[8] In particular, Krueger (1974) assessed the impact of trade barriers on the Indian and Turkish economies. India's import licences, imposed at the behest of its mercantilist manufacturing sector, were found to cost the country in the region of 7 per cent of its annual GNP in 1964, while the equivalent figure for Turkey was 15 per cent in 1968.

[9] As an aside, it is worth noting that self-interest, far from precluding co-operation, in many cases fosters it (see, for example, Dawkins, 1989). For any self-interested individual it is rational to co-operate when the expected discounted benefits of co-operation exceed the expected discounted costs; thus in a repeated two-person game of indeterminate length the best strategy is 'co-operative tit-for-tat' (Axelrod, 1984).

is likely that some people will break their own legs in order to be cared for.

We can see, then, that the existence of 'aid' moneys itself provides an incentive for the autocrat to oppress 'his' people – creating poverty in order that he be eligible for 'aid'. Furthermore, if 'aid' is disbursed according to the degree of deprivation of the population, as it is at present – with only the poorest nations eligible for IDA grants – then the autocrat has a further incentive to deprive 'his' people. In this perverse game, the most oppressive autocrat wins.

Taken together, these insights help explain how political entrepreneurs determine the course of the political process and the consequent allocation and distribution of resources.

The Scramble for Africa and Colonialism

Following the abolition of the slave trade in the late 1840s, commerce between West Africa and Europe began to grow. This led to a heightening of intertribal conflict, as several tribes wrestled for monopoly control over the increasingly lucrative trade routes. At the same time British, French, Portuguese and Dutch traders were engaged in a battle for control of the monopoly to supply Europe with certain valuable commodities.

Between 1876 and 1912 several European governments, at the behest of political entrepreneurs seeking the rents available from the sole supply of commodities and monopoly control of resources, systematically and bloodily dissected the African continent (Pakenham, 1991; Tiffen *et al.*, 1994; Bates, 1984; Ayittey, 1991, 1992).

In theory, 'colonialism was an extractive, generally profitable operation, the objective of which was to maximise revenue at the lowest cost. ... [However, the] profitability of colonialism is now subject to much debate. ... Revenues rarely matched the costs of colonial rule very closely; sometimes they were much higher, other times much lower' (Ayittey, 1992, p. 83). Indeed one study has proclaimed that the 'Belgian Congo was the only colony that paid off directly to a European government' (Curtin *et al.*, 1988, cited by Ayittey, 1992, p.83).

While colonial rule may not have been financially profitable for the treasuries of the colonial governments, it was clearly profitable for those interests whom it served. In Kenya, native farmers were thrown off their land as a result of laws passed by the colonial administration declaring 'unused' land to be 'Crown property' (Tiffen *et al.*, 1994). European farmers then acquired these lands and hired the landless natives at very low wages. In addition, native farmers were prohibited from growing Kenya's most valuable cash crop, coffee, so the European farmers could have a monopoly on its production (Bates, 1984). In South Africa, a series of laws was passed by the colonial administration, at the behest of the owners of mines and other industry, which forced blacks off their lands, and then made it illegal for them to be tenant farmers. The landless blacks thus became cheap labour for the industrialists (Luow and Kendal, 1986; Mbaku, 1991).

While the direct beneficiaries of these racist laws were the European farmers and industrialists who had lobbied for their inception, the administrators themselves also gained. First through the 'perks' of the job; second, by supporting the interests of firms owned by influential Britons, French, and others, the administrators enamoured themselves to the politicians back home (whose chances of re-election had been enhanced).

Neo-Colonialism

During the 1950s, 1960s and 1970s, sometimes peacefully, sometimes following a protracted period of guerrilla warfare, the colonial powers gradually ceded control of the countries they had partitioned in the continent of Africa. But in most African countries, 'independence' turned out to be nothing but a transfer of power from one oppressive régime to another – the leaders of the anti-colonial movement simply assuming power as soon as the colonial administration had moved out (Fieldhouse, 1986; Diamond, 1988; Ayittey, 1992).

As in any autocracy, African leaders had to impose all manner of social controls in order to stay in power. So, for example, the forced migration of millions of Ethiopian peasants during Mengistu's reign (1974-91) served to bolster support for his régime. This was achieved in a number of ways:

• *first*, dislocated, starving and oppressed peasants, their indigenous institutions undermined, were less able to resist the régime;

- *second*, pictures of dislocated and starving peasants, described by Western reporters as the 'victims of famine', generated support for pressure groups such as Oxfam, which in turn called for fiscal money to be spent on food aid to Ethiopia. Much of this aid was subsequently requisitioned by the military élite;

- *third*, the military élite, freed from the necessity of buying food, used tax money to purchase more weapons from the USSR, enabling them further to oppress the peasantry;[10]

- *fourth*, Mengistu used tax money, made available through fungible aid,[11] to purchase all manner of Western luxuries (Scotch whisky, caviar, salmon, lobster and champagne were among the delectables), which he lavished on his junta (Ayittey, 1992, p.108).

The 'Aid' Game

The Ethiopian tragedy is a sad but altogether typical example of a common phenomenon: 'aid', coercively taken from people in developed countries in the form of taxes, is diverted from its intended recipients by corrupt politicians who use it to bolster their oppressive régimes. Similar stories can be told for most African countries.

Whittaker (1988, p. 43) estimated that 'the proportion of African funds going to equip and pay the military has been steadily rising, reaching for example over 40 per cent in Ethiopia, and 25 per cent and 10 per cent in drought-ravaged

---

[10] This is one way in which 'aid' becomes fungible (see below). Between seizing power in 1974 and fleeing Ethiopia in 1991, Mengistu's army, using the $11 billion of weapons supplied by the USSR, carried out a series of 'indiscriminate bombings, shellings, and slaughter of civilians. Even famine relief centres in the north and along the Sudan border were bombed and burned' (Ayittey, 1992, p.107; see also Ayittey, 1991, pp.464-65).

[11] Aid may be diverted from its intended recipients by allocating 'administration' fees (which typically exceed 30 per cent of a project's total cost) to favoured persons or groups (ICHRI, 1985). In addition, aid usurps tax money which is then available for other uses, such as investments in foreign banks (Bauer, 1982; Hancock, 1989; Adams, 1991; Ayittey, 1992). When aid is used in this manner it is said to be fungible.

Mauritania and Mali'. Ayittey (1991, p. 153) notes that 'Sixteen African Countries spent more on arms than they received in aid'.

But these problems are by no means unique to Africa – Lord Bauer (1982, p.93) notes that the Vietnamese government continued to receive foreign aid in 1978 and 1979, long after it had initiated its murderous régime of persecution and compulsory migration, while Pol Pot's Khmer Rouge was still receiving Western 'aid' in 1977, 'at a time when its atrocities were well known in the west'.

Given the uses to which foreign 'aid' has been put, it makes sense to ask why such 'aid' has been given at all.

Multilateral Loans

In July 1944, officials representing 44 of the world's nation states gathered in Bretton Woods, New Hampshire, for the United Nations Monetary and Financial Conference. At this conference, under the chairmanship of John Maynard Keynes, officials agreed to use money taken from taxpayers in the wealthier countries represented to subsidise loans to the governments of the war-ravaged countries of Europe. To facilitate this operation, the International Bank for Reconstruction and Development (IBRD) and the International Monetary Fund (IMF) were set up with a mandate to make loans to governments. In 1949, following Harry S. Truman's Point Four Program, the IBRD and IMF began lending to the governments of 'developing' countries (see also Walters, 1994).

Officials at the United Nations have passed a resolution calling for all developed countries to 'donate'[12] 0·7 per cent of annual GNP towards such 'aid' – this is more than twice the current average level of foreign 'aid donations'. UN officials probably support such initiatives for a number of reasons: to increase their chances of promotion through the bureaucracy (a growing institution offers better job prospects than a shrinking one); to improve their working environment by employing friends and family; and, of course, because they believe that 'aid' disbursed through UN institutions somehow helps the poor in developing countries.

---

[12] 'Donate' is in quotation marks because, of course, this money is taken from tax-payers, that is, the 'donation' is not voluntary.

Bilateral Loans

In addition to contributions to the multilateral 'aid' agencies, state officials of developed countries make loans to state officials of developing countries on a bilateral basis. These loans are usually contingent on the ruling élite of the developing country purchasing some good or service, such as the building contract for the dam being subsidised, from a firm favoured by the ruling élite of the developed country.

There are six primary groups of beneficiaries to this bilateral loan:

- *first*, the firm in the developed country which has lobbied the minister for overseas development to provide the loan;

- *second*, the minister for overseas development, who receives publicity for his benevolent deeds, and hence improves his chances of re-election;[13]

- *third*, the officials in the developing country, who are able to bolster support for their régime by awarding jobs and gifts to strategically important people and to increase spending on the means of oppression (weapons) and perhaps have funds left over for their own Swiss bank account;

- *fourth*, the strategically important people in the developing country who are given jobs and gifts by the officials;

- *fifth*, the 'experts' who advise on the loans and draw up the contracts;

- *sixth*, the NGOs (non-government organisations), which are increasingly the recipients of 'aid' money.

Pressure Groups

Pressure groups such as Oxfam, SOS Sahel and Friends of the Earth constantly exhort their members to lobby state officials in developed countries to increase the level of 'aid' given to the governments of developing countries. A typical example is the

---

[13] He may also obtain some psychic reward from the (largely misplaced) belief that he is doing good.

following from the *Oxfam Campaigner* newsletter (No. 12, Autumn 1994, p.1.):

'ACTION: Write to your MP and ask if s/he will support an increase in the ODA [Overseas Development Administration] budget in this year's public spending round.'

By engaging in such campaigning, without being directly responsible for the disbursement of 'aid' moneys, these pressure groups gain valuable press coverage without suffering from the negative press given to failed 'aid' projects.

A more direct incentive to engage in lobbying (as noted above) is the increasing tendency for 'aid' money to be spent on projects co-ordinated by the NGOs, a tendency which reached new heights with the signing of the Convention on Desertification which assigns NGOs a rôle in designing and implementing national programmes and in overseeing national desertification funds. However, it remains to be seen whether the failure of such expenditures to fend off the spectre of desertification will be blamed on the NGOs. They may well once again blame lack of funds (for an example of this, see Harrison, 1989). So the 'aid' bandwagon rolls on.

Conclusions

This chapter has presented a brief overview of the political evolution of Africa, arguing that many of the actions taken by state officials, in both the developed and developing worlds, have been taken out of concern for their own self-interest, not out of concern for the interests of the people they ostensibly represent. Moreover, transfers of money from taxpayers in developed countries, through 'aid' programmes, have helped to support corrupt and oppressive régimes in developing countries.

5. The Causes of Land Degradation

This chapter outlines the underlying causes of land degradation in Africa.

Indigenous Institutions under Colonialism

Colonialism was an unjust system. In the words of George Ayittey[1] (1991, p. 43) it was 'oppressive, destructive and exploitative'. But its effects have often been exaggerated, for, as Ayittey continues,

'most of Africa's indigenous institutions survived under colonialism. Native courts and legal systems were actually strengthened in the beginning of the colonial period ... The indigenous economic system was generally left intact ... Surplus produce was sold on open, free village markets. Prices on these markets were determined during the colonial era in exactly the same manner as they were determined in pre-colonial times – by bargaining ... [However,] in the political arena ... the indigenous system came into violent clash with colonial rule ... Nevertheless the council of elders was left untouched. Furthermore, the indigenous social structures adapted themselves to enhance their chances of survival under colonialism.'(See also, *inter alia*: Gellar, 1986; Austen, 1987; Manning 1988.)

Indigenous Institutions after Colonialism

Ayittey (1992, p.94) suggests that, with hindsight,

'the task facing African leaders after independence was clear: to develop the traditional sector that the colonialists had neglected, to restore the traditional authority that the chiefs and kings had lost under colonialism and to rebuild the native political structures that the colonialists had tried to destroy'.

---

[1] Ayittey is Professor of Economics at the American University in Washington DC and consultant to the World Bank.

However, the outcome was rarely even close to this ideal. In most countries, the new rulers attempted to convert their lands into model 'socialist' nations. There are several reasons for this:

- *first*, the leaders of the resistance had the 'will to power' – they could see that 'their' people had been mistreated and wished to right these wrongs by imposing their own vision of society upon the people;

- *second*, in the minds of many Africans, especially those members of the élite trained in Marxist economics at Western (and Eastern) universities, colonialism was equated with capitalism, so the logical antidote was socialism;

- *third*, African village life was, and to a large extent still is, very community-oriented, so it was relatively easy to convince Africans that their central government should be 'community-oriented', which is easily confused with 'communist';

- *fourth*, officials in the Soviet Union and the World Bank were willing donors to such régimes because their own central plans for development, representing their own visions for society, could then be put into action.[2]

In a few short years these oppressive régimes succeeded in undermining the indigenous institutions which had enabled peasants and nomads to adapt to changing circumstances, institutions which even the colonial rulers had left more or less intact.

Indigenous political systems were replaced by dictatorships, in which local units of government became irrelevant. Market systems were replaced by central planning: government boards were established to purchase and sell all goods – the middleman, the entrepreneur, was eliminated and with him the opportunity to bargain, setting prices according to supply and demand.

---

[2] As Andrew Warren (personal communication) noted: these expenditures were often justified to national governments on the grounds that they contributed to the international battle between 'capitalism' and 'communism' (which was also played out in a more direct way, through the supply of weapons and military training).

Land Reforms

One of the most significant changes made by African dictators, and one of the few changes which continues to attract widespread support from academics in the developed world, was 'land reform' – whereby land accumulated by a minority of political entrepreneurs was redistributed among the peasants.

While it would seem just that land taken by force should be returned to its rightful owner, it is doubtful whether 'the state' is the appropriate administrator of such a process. Summing up the evidence on the impact of land reform policies around the world, Powelson and Stock (1990, p.12) are not enthusiastic:

> 'Land reform – much needed in the Third World for both equity and efficiency – has become one of the instruments by which the "agricultural surplus" (amounts produced by farmers above subsistence) has been skimmed off by the state, ostensibly to promote economic development. The resources are often misused, however, through either direct corruption or extravagant, wasteful projects to promote the political or territorial interests of powerful people. Usually land reform agencies are manipulated to serve the urban bias in government policy. Furthermore, the imposition of state-sponsored programs upon village people destroys village cultures and institutions, preventing them from developing rationally as circumstances require.'

An Institutional Problem – The World Bank

Jeffrey Sachs[3] (1994, p.31), puts at least some of the blame for the failure of these land reforms (and other programmes) on the World Bank: 'The Bank's greatest failure in the past has been to support the cock-eyed schemes of African despots.' But Bank officials did more than just support these 'cock-eyed schemes', they often dictated them: The Bank's 1975 statement on agricultural policy insisted that the efficient allocation of resources necessitated:

> 'the packaging of credit together with extension and infrastructure ... All components of a [World Bank] production package should be, and usually are, financed under such schemes ... Clearly there is a

---

[3] Sachs is Professor of Economics at Harvard University and a consultant to the World Bank.

need to think of production packages for the farm as an entity and to finance all complementary components ... To make the credit programme a success the government must provide the complementary inputs ... The package approach is to be preferred since it provides the farmer with credit plus all the ancillary services he requires' (World Bank, 1975, Agricultural Sector Policy Paper, quoted by Goodell, 1990, p.17).

No doubt officials at the World Bank uttered these sentiments in good faith, believing that private money lenders, seed growers and pesticide manufacturers were charging extortionary rates for their services, while private purchasers 'unfairly' varied the price they paid for the farmers' output according to the vagaries of international demand. However, these officials were too myopic to foresee the perverse effects of their recommendations – that state officials would implement the reforms in a self-interested manner, rather than in a way that served the interests of the peasants, and that central planning is simply incapable of meeting the wants of the people.[4]

In a subsequent confidential internal report, World Bank officials were deeply critical of the earlier reforms, but treated this 'as merely a technical matter or, worse yet, as the fault of the extension service or of farmers' ignorance' (Goodell, 1990, p.23). Planners in the Bank, the IMF, USAID, and elsewhere on the 'aid' bandwagon, intent on imposing their own vision of society upon the poor of the developing world, simply refuse to accept the blame for their wrongdoing. A psychologist might diagnose cognitive dissonance: the more the planners are criticised, the more they believe in the necessity of 'aid'.[5]

Intervention Failure and Land Degradation

Begun by despots and supported by 'aid' agencies, the attempt to plan African economies centrally, from Somalia to Sudan, has led to corruption, waste and, perhaps most seriously, the breakdown of the indigenous institutions (see Box 1 below).

---

[4] It is sad to reflect that this was known in the 1920s: see Mises (1951).

[5] It has to be said that scepticism is not entirely absent within the Bank. Following a number of particularly savage attacks published to coincide with the Bank's 50th anniversary (for example, Rich, 1994; Bandow and Vasquez, 1994), the president, fearing a drop in staff morale, circulated a collection of pro-Bank newspaper articles.

Discussed below are some of the interventions into the lives of peasants and nomads which have led to land degradation.

1. Restrictions on the Ownership of Land

The leaders of many African countries have placed severe restrictions on the private ownership of property. Such restrictions, especially when land is 'owned' by the state, reduce the individual peasant's incentive and ability to invest in land.[6] Under state management, the people who decide how the land is used (the bureaucrats) do not receive the full benefits from improvements made to it (such as the future output of improved land), or the full costs of not making such improvements (such as loss of top soil and, hence, future harvests). This results in a 'tragedy of the collective', in which too few resources are invested in the land, leading to soil erosion, deflation, salinisation and other processes involved in land degradation.

Under state ownership and private management, peasants will reinvest less in the land than they would if they owned it. Such a régime fosters the problem known as the 'tragedy of the commons',[7] in which competing users of a piece of land, unhindered by custom or law, deplete the nutrients of that land more rapidly than would take place if the land were managed by a single authority with incentives to preserve it (see Box 2 below).

2. State-Subsidised Boreholes

Across arid Africa, States have subsidised (often with 'aid' money) the drilling of boreholes, creating thousands of mini oases. Peasants and nomads flock to these boreholes to take advantage of the 'free' (unowned and unpriced) water and land. Nomadic pastoralists are even induced into becoming sedentary, and therefore more easily controlled by the state (Thomas &

---

6 Under such circumstances, peasants will have less incentive to invest in their land because they will be less secure about how much of the harvest will accrue to them, and they will be less able to make such an investment because it will be more difficult to obtain credit, since they have less property to act as security against a loan.

7 Without entering into the sterile debate between Hardin and Monbiot (see *Scientific American*, January and February 1994), suffice to say that by 'commons' we in fact mean land under open access (see Box 2 below).

BOX 1:

The Tragedy of Central Planning

Africa was not the only place where such savagery was inflicted upon the people. The nightmare of attempted central planning in the former USSR has been well documented (see, for example, Bernstam, 1990, for a review of the ecological consequences). Grace Goodell (1990, pp.22-23), an anthropologist at Johns Hopkins University, eloquently describes the Masagana 99 (land reform) experiment in the Philippines:

'[Under] Masagana 99 [the state] offered low-interest loans – 12 per cent per season – that undercut the private market's 50 per cent or higher... Since a private farmer can draw his Masagana loan from only the one bank or credit program appointed to his village ... he has no choice on which one to patronise and no opportunity to play off agencies against each other for better services.

'Thus, Masagana 99 insulates its borrowers from the dangers of greedy private moneylenders, but not from the state itself. Loans may be issued only through the state-controlled 'farmers' co-operatives' (in quotation marks because they were not formed at the farmers' initiative); official lending agencies are strictly assigned to prevent farmers from shopping around; loans are subject to fixed government rates and regulations ... and the state's technical recommendations, state controlled inputs, and often state procurement policies attempt to determine all farming operations so far as is possible...

'"Planters" Products [not the real name], financed and granted monopoly operations by the state and owned by government élites, has taken over almost all agricultural supply stores in the country ... All private retail chains for farm supplies have been extinguished. No longer do independent salesmen bring to the farmers the challenges of alternative inputs. The Chinese middlemen have been driven underground; private seed growers have been forced into the state's association for them; all rice millers and traders are circumscribed within the state's procurement and pricing policies; and the state reserves a monopoly on exporting rice...

'The sharp reduction in seasonal price variation, due to government intervention, has eroded the private sector's profit margins so that it is less able to finance post-harvest facilities, such as processing and storing. And so the state intervenes further.'

Goodell (1990, p.23) continues with a truly Kafkaesque description of the impact of state intervention:

'Farmers are now worse off than they were under the landlords. To settle a disagreement over a loan, a peasant must penetrate the central bank of the Philippines, a maze of corridors in downtown Manila. To argue over the price of Carburofan, he must seek out the National Food and Agriculture Council, somewhere within the Ministry of Agriculture, itself somewhere within the government complex, somewhere in distant Quezon City.'

Middleton, 1994, p.89). These peasants and nomads then overuse the 'free' water and land, resulting in a 'tragedy of the commons'.[8]

In contrast, when a family drills a borehole on its own land, it can choose whether to allow others to use its water or not, thereby ensuring sustainable use of the land around the borehole. In addition, if both the land and the underground water are privately owned, owners would be able to co-operate with each other to manage the water reserves sustainably (for example, through the use of contingent contracts[9]).

3. State-Subsidised Dams

Encouraged and financed by 'aid' agencies, and especially the World Bank, the leaders of nations across Africa have spent billions of dollars on dams, the effects of which have often been horrific (Adams, 1991). By preventing the natural flow of water, dams often flood regions of useful land, creating lakes which become breeding grounds for disease-ridden insects (Operations Evaluations Department, 1989). In addition, dams sequester the mineral-rich silt, thereby reducing the quality of the soil on downstream floodplains.[10] The farmers on these floodplains, often unaware of the impact of the dam, continue to farm their

---

[8] Mortimore (1990) suggests that in some cases, perhaps because of the superabundence of land in certain areas, and elsewhere through the application of coping strategies, these problems are not as acute as this paragraph suggests. In other cases they clearly are.

[9] Water can be managed as a 'club' good (Buchanan, 1965). Individuals who wish to extract water from an aquifer each sign a contingent contract stating that they will extract no more than a specified quantity of water; this contract only becomes binding once a certain proportion of users has signed up. However, once this threshold is reached, anyone reneging on the contract can be fined by the other signatories (see also, Ostrom, 1988, 1990). Note that for such contracts to be viable, a cheap method of dispute resolution is needed. State law is rarely cheap (or equitable), so it would seem to be desirable to allow private law merchants (Benson, 1990).

[10] Mahmood (1987) estimates that approximately one per cent of a reservoir's capacity is filled by sediment every year. Apart from the magnitude of the problem for downstream farmers which this implies, the utility of the dam is surely called into question (and the myth that dams would be worth building if only we took a longer-term view is dispelled).

land intensively, and consequently deplete their soils.[11] Some dams have turned out to be giant white elephants.[12]

4. State Subsidies to Irrigation and Mechanised Farming

One of the principal purposes of these dams (apart from producing pointlessly large quantities of electricity – another subsidy to favoured Western industries) was to irrigate the arid lands of Africa. The sadly unforeseen consequence of such irrigation schemes have often been as bad as those resulting from the dam itself. In many areas the water table has risen, which in turn has increased the salinity of the soil, making it unsuitable for many crops. In the long-run this leads to land degradation (Umali, 1993; see also Figure 1, below, p.76).[13]

Furthermore, states often subsidise farm machinery (usually bought from manufacturers in 'donor' countries). Once purchased, however, these machines are commonly simply left to rot: farmers realise that the cost of using a machine outweighs its benefits, either because the fuel it consumes is too costly, or because the machinery requires servicing by skilled mechanics, a rare commodity in Africa.

State subsidies to irrigation and to mechanised farming benefit the recipients of the water, tractors and combine harvesters, at the cost of the peasant farmer, who must pay. Irrigation of large farms means less water for small farms; subsidised machinery on large farms means fewer peasants are employed, and wage rates are lower. Subsidies are paid for directly by the peasant, who must sell his produce to the state-run agriculture board at below-market rates.

---

[11] For example, a dam across the Ganges in Southern India has led to a reduction in deposits of silt on the river's delta in Bangladesh. This has resulted in widespread soil erosion in the delta area and many peasants have become landless.

[12] As Warren and Khogali (1992) note: 'The South Lake Chad scheme in Nigeria, to have been fed by pumps from the lake, is now stranded hundreds of kilometres from its intended source.'

[13] Irrigation schemes need not always be bad: they can bring water to undernourished soils and reduce the salinising impact of floodwater. However, grand irrigation schemes, subsidised by the state and benefitting a few wealthy farmers rarely satisfy the wants of peasants and nomads.

BOX 2:

The Tragedy of the Commons

In his *Politics*, Aristotle said:

> 'that which is common to the greatest number has the least good bestowed upon it. Every one thinks chiefly of his own, hardly at all of the common interest; and only when he is himself concerned as an individual. For besides other considerations, everybody is more inclined to neglect the duty which he expects another to fulfil.'

If it is the case that individuals do think chiefly of their own interests, then it is important that the institutional framework within which they operate reflects that fact.

Thus, if 10 men all graze their cattle on the same piece of land, each man realises that any land he does not graze his cattle on will be used by another, so he has a strong incentive to graze as much of the available land as possible. Stated in reverse: no man has a strong incentive to graze fewer than the maximum number of cattle he can afford. Such a system of grazing, called 'open access', will inevitably lead to what Hardin called 'the tragedy of the commons' (Hardin, 1968), that is, the cattle will denude the land and, in the absence of free land to move the cattle onto, the cattle will die. Historically, open access has been a rarity, occurring only when land is so plentiful that ownership is not necessary, or, as in Africa, when political entrepreneurs deny individuals their right to property.[1]

Under a system of private ownership, individuals may only graze cattle on their own land, or on the land of others by contractual agreement. Thus, individuals have an incentive to conserve the land, grazing only the number of cattle their land can support. Those who fail to do so will soon cease to be cattle ranchers.[2] Thus, Nicholas Wade (1974) noted:

---

[1] In many societies, political entrepreneurs have enforced private land ownership using the state's monopoly of power - often (as in Europe since the 16th century) transferring common land into the hands of the political entrepreneurs, such as the Lords and Princes. Prior to these interventions, access to the commons was restricted by peasants' *de facto* ownership of land, with disputes over rights of use settled by the local protection agency (church or lord) (Berman, 1982). (For Africa, see Ault and Rutman, 1979; Mbaku, 1991.)

[2] For ease of exposition, only two forms of access to land have been delineated here: open access and private property. However, the meaning of 'private' property should be clarified: in the sense in which it is used here, private property means property for which an identifiable person or group of people is (are) the principal 'residual claimant(s)', see Barzel (1990). Residual claimants have a right to any good produced by that property, and are liable for any externalities generated. Many fascinating alternative mechanisms for managing property, especially where individual rights are difficult to delineate, are discussed in Elinor Ostrom (1988, 1990) and Schlager and Ostrom (1992).

'Norman H. Macleod, an agronomist at the American University in Washington, DC ... found ... that the difference between [a pentagon of green land in the Sahel – spotted on a satellite photo –] and the surrounding desert was nothing more than barbed-wire fence. Within was a 250,000-acre ranch, divided into five sectors with the cattle allowed to graze one sector a year. Although the ranch was started only five years ago, at the same time as the drought began, the simple protection afforded the land was enough to make the difference between pasture and desert.'

In addition, the institution of private property gives people an incentive to invent new technologies, because individuals know that they will be the principal beneficiaries of any investments they make in research and development. So, for example, growing fodder to feed cattle enables peasants to farm more intensively because less land is required during the winter or dry seasons.

It is likely that, before the tragedy occurs (and even more so once it has begun), an entrepreneur would see the advantage of dividing up the common land into individual plots. If people are free to pursue the courses of action they choose (subject to the caveat that in so doing they do not hinder the ability of another to pursue the course of action he chooses), then this entrepreneur is likely to succeed in dividing up the land in a way in which everybody benefits; in an African tribe this might be done through the village assembly. This division is expected to occur when the costs of exclusion (that is, the costs of limiting access to a piece of previously open land, for example by fencing and policing) are equal to or less than the external costs (which, in this case, means the costs associated with the denudation of the land) (Alchian, 1965; Demsetz, 1967; Anderson and Hill, 1975; Ault and Rutman, 1979).

However, the costs of exclusion will depend upon the exclusion technologies available. Wherever there are externalities present, we would expect that individuals will have an incentive to produce new and cheaper exclusion technologies. So, over time, we would expect more and more land to become privately owned and the sum of external costs to decline precipitously.

Exclusion is not the only technology which individuals can adapt and innovate. Entrepreneurial peasants constantly introduce new crops and production methods, creating an environment of diverse agriculture (Brookfield and Padoch, 1994). Technological innovation not only enables peasants to improve their lot, it also benefits those with whom they trade by lowering the cost of purchasing food and other goods and reducing the risk of famine. But agrodiversity will be stifled if those who might innovate new technologies are not allowed to benefit from the investments they make through the ownership of property. The individual's *incentive* to *invest* in his land and *innovate* new methods of production will be greater when he can *own* and *exchange property*. Thus, Michael Stahl (1993) concludes:

'At the farm level, the presence or absence of clearly defined property rights makes the difference between active interest in investing in soil conservation measures or apparent indifference to environmental degradation.'

5. Compulsory Resettlement Programmes and Compulsory Limits on Livestock Ownership

Across the Sahel, states have enacted compulsory resettlement programmes, through which peasants and nomads have been moved away from their land, either because their land was to be flooded by a state- subsidised dam, or simply at the whim of a dictator. Such programmes create uncertainty over the ownership of land (even where individuals are *de jure* barred from owning land this is a problem, since *de facto* ownership becomes unenforceable), leading to a reduction in the incentive to invest in land improvements. In addition, peasants and nomads are usually moved onto less fertile land, for which their farming methods are not well adapted, so they unwittingly erode the soil.

One policy which African dictators learned from colonial agriculturists (via planners at the World Bank) was the imposition of compulsory limits on the ownership of cattle. The argument for limiting ownership of cattle goes as follows: peasants/nomads see cattle as a sign of wealth and will therefore hoard more cattle than the land can support, so by limiting the number of cattle which can be owned, peasants/nomads will be saved from their own greed and the inevitable population crash resulting from the 'tragedy of the commons'. What this argument omits is that in many instances the grazing of cattle is limited by customary right, so that more important individuals will graze more cattle by right not (only) greed. More importantly, cattle are used as drought food: during times of rain, individuals in arid areas build up stocks of cattle which are then milked, bled, consumed, or sold during times of drought. In addition, cattle are able to eat a greater diversity of naturally occurring grasses than are humans and so enable pastoralists to move to where the rains fall. In very arid areas, where rainfall is sporadic, the ability to move to the rains is an important coping strategy.[14] By stealing cattle in the name of 'rational management', state officials consign individuals to malnutrition (and, in the process, make them reliant upon the state).[15]

---

[14] For a fascinating discussion of the coping strategies of one such group of pastoralists, the Ariaal of Northern Kenya, see Fratkin (1991).

[15] Where customary tenure has been insufficient restraint on the ownership of cattle, so that a tragedy of the commons has resulted, peasants ofen have alternative coping

6. The Knowledge Problem

A more general problem with state intervention is its intrinsic inability to meet the needs of the people. This is a consequence of 'the knowledge problem'. Only an individual knows his own needs and wants, and these are best satisfied through mutually advantageous exchanges in the market (Hayek, 1945). When political entrepreneurs receive a non-market transfer from people trading in the market (through taxes, licences and regulations), or provide a transfer to such traders (a subsidy) the prices of goods in the market are distorted – they no longer represent what people would be willing to pay for them through uncoerced exchange. As a result, people's needs and wants are no longer met as effectively.

Figure 1 (below) presents a flow diagram showing how intervention failure leads to a vicious circle of land degradation, aid, and oppression.

Anti-Desertification Failures

It has been estimated that between 1978 and 1983, four multilateral agencies (the World Bank, FAO, UNESCO and UNEP) spent $10 billion on projects 'said to have a desertification component' (Thomas & Middleton, 1994, p.64). Of this $10 billion, only around 10 per cent went on field projects to control desertification, while the rest was spent on more general aid programmes (such as land reform, irrigation projects and reforestation schemes), and over 30 per cent of this was spent on administration (*ibid.*). The efficacy of these 'anti-desertification' projects has been called into question: Thomas and Middleton (1994, p.64), the authors of UNEP's World Atlas of Desertification, have noted that 'some of these projects, such as those aimed at reducing animal losses and digging more wells, may even make the situation worse'.

Most 'anti-desertification' projects in the past relied upon technocratic 'solutions': mechanical earth movers were used to build soil-retentive terraces; grasses were planted in an attempt to fix dunes; trees were planted to reafforest denuded areas.

---

strategies, such as switching to the grazing of goats, which are able to eat acacia (see Chapter 2).

FIGURE 1: The Political Economy of Land Degradation

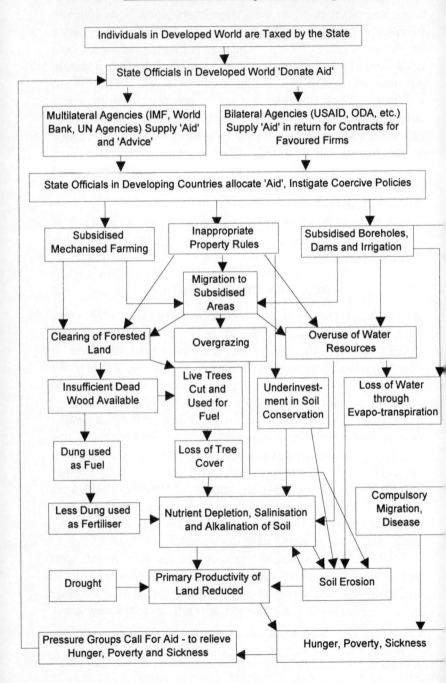

These projects typically ignored the wants of the people affected: indigenous people usually build terraces for their water-retentive properties to improve crop output; indigenous people do not attempt to 'fix' dunes because moving house is cheaper; reafforestation is pointless in areas where all the trees are owned by the state, since the indigenous people have insufficient incentive to care for the growing trees (which soon become firewood) (Warren and Khogali, 1992, pp.55-73).

There are some signs that the interests of indigenous people are beginning to be recognised by those responsible for funding antidesertification projects, for example, there has been a shift to funding projects through NGOs – which at least see the importance of grass-roots action. However, this shift in funding is at best a marginal improvement, since the central problems remain: state officials in developing countries (and particularly in Africa) continue to restrict the freedom of individuals to own property, to engage in uncoerced exchange and to resolve disputes through customary law. Spending on 'antidesertification' projects under such circumstances can at best produce short-term solutions, and at worst is counterproductive because attention is focused away from the real problem.

Amongst the plethora of projects with 'a desertification component' (that is, those included in national plans of action to combat desertification) have been agro-forestry projects, water resource management and development, range management, and soil and water conservation (Warren and Khogali, 1992, p.55). Critical assessments of such projects are rather hard to find: any project which is less than an abject failure according to its own remit seems to receive applause from the self-seeking bureaucrats who write the appraisals. However, if one reads between the lines a different picture emerges. Noted below are two examples of such projects.

First, an afforestation programme in Nyerere's Tanzania, intended to reduce soil erosion, was a model of bureaucratic blundering. According to a World Bank report, 'little attention has been paid to minimising costs' (Blackwell *et al.*, 1991, p.63) – for example, fertiliser was brought in from afar when local sources were cheaper. Even the rationale for the afforestation programme was flawed, since coppicing of existing trees would have been cheaper.[16] These blunders are at least partly the result of the complexity of the chains of communication between those paying for the conservation schemes and those carrying them out:

> 'Village forestry activities in Tanzania are implemented and financed through the regional administrative structure of the country. Funds are channelled through the Treasury to the prime minister's office (PMO); then to the districts (Natural Resources Officer); and finally to Division Forest Officers, who pay the labourers, the nursery works, and other costs for village forestry. The technical and financial reporting follow a reverse flow' (Blackwell *et al.*, 1991, p.63).

These chains of command were praised in the report (perhaps out of admiration for Nyerere's socialist vision), but must surely have reduced the quality and quantity of information being transmitted between those who want firewood and those able to supply it. If the forests were privately owned, and the exchange of wood for other goods allowed without state intervention, this information would have been conveyed much more effectively (through the price mechanism), allowing individual wants to be better met.

Second, the Sudanese government has spent over $1 billion, including World Bank loans of over $450 million, irrigating 1·1 million hectares of arid land. One of the largest schemes, the Roseires irrigation project, a 60-metre high dam, built in 1961 at a cost of $111 million, trapped 2·7m cubic metres of water and supplied 184,000 hectares of cropland.[17] However, a report for

---

[16] A coppice is created by chopping a tree down to a small stump. This then sprouts many fine branches, which are an excellent source of wood for fires. Coppices generate wood at a much faster rate than other forestry techniques. However, if people are to grow coppices, rather than chop down trees, they must have an incentive to do so – such as the right to future ownership of the coppiced wood.

[17] Admittedly, the Roseires project preceded the 'antidesertification' campaign, but it is nevertheless a salutary lesson in how not to solve water resource problems. A later project in South Darfur Privince, Sudan, which 'was planned as the first stage of a 12-year program to reverse a perceived ecological deterioration in the area by instituting changes in customary land use practises', could certainly be said to have had an 'antidesertification' component, and was described quite simply as 'a failure' (Operations Evaluation Department, 1989, p.168).

the Operations Evaluations Department of the World Bank concluded that:

> '[T]he storage capacity of the reservoir proved to be excessive by 80 per cent because the irrigable area had been overestimated ... the area irrigated was poorly utilised because not enough attention had been given to production packages, incentives, and co-ordination of the use of the Nile waters for power and irrigation ... potential dangers to the health of the population arose because of malaria and schistosomiasis [both carried by insects which bred in the reservoir] ... and ...the nomads who were displaced from the reservoir and newly irrigated areas suffered' (Operations Evaluations Department, 1989).

Here, the evaluators seem to accord almost equal weight to the (admittedly dramatic) failure of the reservoir to meet expectations and the serious intervention into the lives of the individuals living nearby, implying that World Bank officials are employing some kind of utilitarian calculus: weighing up the costs of one life against the benefits to another. The fact that the dam failed to meet the needs of the people just makes this calculus seem absurd. Of course the reason for this failure is the same as for the failure of the afforestation programme in Tanzania (and most other World Bank projects, for that matter): central planning does not work.

By 1992, over 500 projects with 'an antidesertification component' had been enacted, the vast majority in Africa (Odingo, 1992, p.9). Each year around $1 billion is spent in this fashion (EarthAction Newsletter, October 1994). Yet in 1990 Mostafa Tolba, then secretary-general of UNEP, called the outcome of this binge of 'anti-desertification' spending, 'pathetic' (quoted by Pearce, 1992, p.39).

Taken individually, some projects seem to have been successful[18] (although one might well ask: compared to what?),

---

[18] Warren and Khogali (1992, pp.72-3), note of the project in the Yatenga region of Burkina Faso:

'Yatenga was a badly degraded area in the early 1980s ... [but] once the peasants appreciated the value of the new techniques [which were adapted from indigenous conservation techniques practised elsewhere, such as building stone lines and planting fruit trees] there was spontaneous diffusion of the idea ... Not only do these but the majority, typically based on top-down technocratic solutions, have had limited success[19] and many, especially those which were part of 'development' programmes,[20] have been counterproductive (see above).

A Union Netting Excess Pay-offs

As Chapter 1 shows, UNEP officials played a key rôle in the evolution of the concept of desertification. Mostafa Tolba organised two conferences devoted exclusively to its discussion; he also co-ordinated the Plan of Action to Combat Desertification, which has been responsible, directly and indirectly, for the disbursement of billions of dollars to corrupt politicians in the developing world. The authors of a Greenpeace report, Warren and Agnew (1988, pp.7-8), are succinct:

> 'Desertification has become an "institutional fact" ... one that an institution wanted to believe, one that served its purposes.'

Thomas and Middleton (1994, p. 161), the authors of the UNEP *World Atlas of Desertification,* elaborate:

> 'The United Nations has played a major rôle in conceptualising desertification since 1977. It could be considered to have created desertification, the institutional myth. It has been the source of publicity that has frequently had little reliable scientific foundation. The success of UN-derived anti- desertification measures have yet to be reliably demonstrated and, in many cases appear to have had little relevance to affected peoples. Without the UN, desertification may not be as high on the environmental agenda as it is today.'

---

techniques increase yields on already cultivated fields, but they can bring back land into production.'

[19] As Warren and Khogali (1992, p.73) note:

'The most salutary lesson from Yatenga is that only techniques fitted to local environmental and social conditions will succeed. When an attempt to introduce stone lines similar to those that were so successful at Yatenga was made in the Affole mountains in Mauritania, the successes were much more modest.'

[20] Recommendation 22 of the PACD actually stated that programmes to combat desertification *should* be part of national development plans.

That the officials at UNEP have benefited from the myth they created is beyond doubt.[21] However, the number of projects run jointly by UNEP and other UN agencies and affiliates attests to the level of rent-seeking behaviour in the UN as a whole. This rent-seeking has led to large-scale financial support for oppressive régimes – régimes which have denied people the right to property, the right to customary law, and the right to exchange goods freely. In turn, these interventions have led to people being less willing and less able to invest in improvements to their land. In short, the UN has become a Union Nurturing Erosion and Poverty.

Conclusions

This chapter has tried to separate the myths of desertification from the realities.

The myth runs as follows:

individuals in the developing world do not understand the environment in which they live, they irrationally graze too many cattle and have too many babies, thereby overgrazing and overcultivating their own land. If this is allowed to continue, these ignorant peasants will destroy the land – turning it to desert.

This myth was created by colonial agriculturists, expanded by USAID officials, fostered by UNEP officials, supported by self-interested officials in 'aid' agencies, and perpetuated by politicians and the media.

---

[21] Between 1977 and 1984, UNEP expenditure on 'combating' desertification was $16,690,026, just under 10 per cent of its total budget (UNEP DC/PAC, 1984). Of this, almost 20 per cent went to administration, while the remainder went to 25 'anti-desertification' projects. Of these 25 projects: five predated UNCOD; one 'concerned the development of a rigorous methodology for the assessment of mapping desertification', involved UNEP, FAO, UNESCO, WMO and ISS (the International Society of Soil Science) and cost nearly $700,000; another was a training programme for government officials; three were training programmes for soil scientists; three involved 'transnational' project support; and the remainder 'involved support for various seminars, conferences and institutional support within the UN' (Thomas & Middleton, 1994, p.37).

The reality is altogether a different story:

Self-seeking autocrats in developing countries undermine the institutions (property rights, customary law and the market) which have enabled peasants to adapt to changing environments. These autocrats then call for 'aid' money to help 'their' people overcome the resultant starvation and 'desertification'. Self-seeking state officials in the developed world, acceding to the demands of pressure groups, then take money from the electorate and disburse it as 'aid'. Upon receipt of this 'aid' money, the autocrat commences a binge of lavish spending on his followers and on weapons with which he oppresses 'his' people. So the cycle continues.

6. Overcoming Oppression

In this chapter a number of means are suggested by which the causal nexus of land degradation, poverty and oppression, identified in Chapter 5, can be broken.

Why Intervention Has Failed

In the 1970s, UNEP's concept of land degradation centred on its immediate causes: nutrient depletion, salinisation, alkalisation of soil and soil erosion (see Figure 1). In response, large, capital intensive 'antidesertification' projects were mounted.

In the 1980s, many blamed the failure of these projects on the technologies adopted: earth movers were used to build terraces in areas where labour would have been far cheaper; grasses were planted on sand dunes at enormous expense, while thousands starved because they had been sold inappropriate fertilisers by the government agriculture board; irrigation schemes made the desert blossom, temporarily, but left the delta bereft of nutrients. In response, such people advocated alternative solutions: more 'grass-roots' action; better development plans. Such policies are promoted in the Convention on Desertification, which obliges 'affected parties', on the one hand to 'prepare a national action programme ... to combat desertification', (Article 9(1)) and, on the other, to 'facilitate the participation of local populations' (Article 5(d)).

While grass-roots action may be desirable (for example, if it strengthens the institutions which help the peasants adapt to their environment), it is inconsistent with the notion of centralised development planning. The chains of command which central plans require mean that information concerning the wants of peasants will be lost – replaced by the wants of the plans' administrators.[1]

---

[1] See Chapter 5 and, for example, Larson (1994), who notes that the World Bank has suggested that all countries should develop NEAPs (National Environmental Action Programmes) in order to be eligible for IDA credits and concludes that 'it is perhaps unrealistic to hope that NEAPs ... can provide a framework for both understanding

As this paper demonstrates, 'experts' have persistently failed to identify correctly the institutional dysfunctions causing land degradation. When, in the 1980s, World Bank officials began to realise that the institutions they had promoted were failing to deliver the goods, they began to encourage 'privatisation'. However, 'privatisation' is not, *per se*, the answer, especially when it is imposed on the peasants, at the behest of World Bank and IMF officials, by autocratic régimes. In these circumstances, 'privatisation' may destroy the very institutions which have enabled the peasants to survive.[2]

Lady Thatcher was wrong when she proclaimed that 'We have to try to teach them the basics of long-term husbandry' (quoted by Hancock, 1989, p.22). As we saw in Chapter 1, attempts to teach 'the natives' how to live have been in process since time immemorial, and the results are all too visible.

Why Reform Will Not Work

Professor Jeffrey Sachs, the Harvard economist, proclaimed in *The Economist* that:

'Dozens of countries, mainly in sub-Saharan Africa, are in such desperate straits that disease, civil unrest and collapsing infrastructure are overwhelming the capacities of economic policy-makers. These countries need more active and effective international support, best led by the World Bank...

'Large scale aid (beyond emergency relief) should be provided only to those countries ready to improve their governance through

---

and alleviating a country's key environmental problems'. This was because 'key underlying factors driving specific environmental problems – creating the "incentives" for "degradation" – were generally not identified. Those that were identified were probably not amenable to change by a NEAP' (p.371).

2 On this point see, for example, Bromley (1991). Note, however, that this is a very different argument from that made by Monbiot (1994) who claims that 'when the commons are privatized, they pass into the hands of people whose priority is to make money ... [and] as the land is no longer the sole means of survival but an investment that can be exchanged, the new owners can overexploit and reinvest elsewhere'. Does not the owner of a piece of land have a strong incentive to conserve and improve that land, in order that its value increase? As Smith (1776) argued, both the profit motive and the tendency to 'truck, barter and exchange' tend to promote the social good (how can voluntary exchange be bad?). It is the imposition of 'order' by a 'leviathan' which is bad: state registration of land which enables an outsider to evict the *de facto* owner of land can destroy the social order built around customary tenure.

political and economic liberalisation. For such countries, however, the aid should be ample and timely.'

While these proposals sound promising on the surface, they belie one of the central themes of Sachs's essay: that the international capital markets are so liquid that, in general, if a project is worth doing, private finance is available and so will flow. It is sufficient to observe that over the past few years the merest hint of political and economic liberalisation in developing countries, from Argentina to Estonia, has made merchant bankers giddy with 'emerging market' fever.[3]

In addition, all the multilateral and bilateral 'aid' organisations, as well as most of the United Nations bodies (such as UNEP, UNDP and FAO), have institutionalised inefficiency – they abound with rent-seekers 'doing lunch' with political entrepreneurs. So it is clear that reform of these institutions, while perhaps an improvement on the current state of affairs, would only be the messiest of compromises. As Sir Alan Walters (1994) has noted of the IMF and the World Bank, '... the ideal solution would be to abolish the Fund and the Bank – wind them up and disperse their expertise to other activities'.

Graham Hancock (1989, pp.192-93), former East Africa correspondent for *The Economist*, has suggested the dissolution of all the offending institutions:

'To continue with the charade seems to me absurd. Garnered and justified in the name of the destitute and the vulnerable, aid's main function in the past half century has been to create and then entrench a powerful new class of rich and privileged people. In that notorious club of parasites and hangers-on made up of the United Nations, the World Bank, and the bilateral agencies, it is aid – and nothing else – that has permitted hundreds of thousands of "jobs for the boys" and that has permitted record breaking standards to be set in self-serving behaviour, arrogance, paternalism, moral cowardice, and mendacity. At the same time, in the developing countries, aid has perpetuated the rule of the incompetent and venal men whose leadership would otherwise be utterly non-viable; it has allowed governments characterised by historic ignorance, avarice, and

---

[3] Of past attempts to impose reform from outside, Gibbon (1992, p.50) notes: 'the [structural] adjustment problemmatic assumes the presence of structures and conditions at variance to African realities. As a result the main beneficiaries of adjustment tend to be the forces it ostensibly sets out to subvert.'

irresponsibility to thrive; last but not least, it has condoned – and in some cases facilitated – the most consistent and grievous abuses of human rights that have occurred anywhere in the world since the dark ages.

'In these closing years of the twentieth century the time has come for the lords of poverty to depart.'

Mechanics of a Solution

Subsidies to entrenched special interest groups are, by their very nature, difficult to remove. The special interests groups working for and benefiting from the UN, the World Bank and the bilateral 'aid' organisations are very deeply entrenched indeed. But subsidies to such interest groups have been removed in the past, viz. the reduction in the size of New Zealand's welfare state, which no longer subsidises the middle classes to anything like the extent that it did; the downfall of the communist dictatorship in Russia – overthrown by the people it oppressed, but with the support of the incumbent dictator; and the privatisation of nationalised industries the world over – despite resistance from those likely to lose their jobs and potential influence. No general theory is available which can explain how or why all these changes occurred. But it seems evident that they would not have been possible without the willing support of the people who benefited. So perhaps it is true to say that the larger the loss and the larger the number of losers from any policy, the higher the chance of that policy being thrown out.[4]

Losses can occur in both pecuniary and psychological terms: taxes are, primarily, a financial loss (but, for some, a psychological gain); while the death of a loved one is primarily a psychological loss (but, for some, a financial gain). Clearly, the loss of a few pence each week in taxes going on 'aid' is not a large inducement to write letters to one's MP, or to organise a 'rally against aid'. However, when a person understands that 'aid' harms the poor in developing nations, the psychological cost to that person of spending his money on 'aid' may also be high, increasing his desire to stop this immoral transfer.

---

[4] Mbaku and Paul (1989) show that high government spending and iniquitous distribution of income increase the chances of a dictator being ousted.

If pro 'aid' pressure groups were to adopt an anti 'aid' stance, they might redress some of the harm they have done.[5] Directors of these pressure groups might even find such a change of tack to be in their interests. The pressure groups could benefit financially – why not urge people to give their money to charities rather than have it taken by the state for use in 'aid' programmes? If oppressive régimes are starved of external sources of cash, they will turn to their own people. But a régime which wishes to remain in power must become accountable to its people, it must reduce the level of corruption, of rent-seeking, and of intervention, or it will be constantly under threat of revolution (Mbaku and Paul, 1989).[6] When the 'aid' organisations stop financing oppressors, the peasants can once again begin to create the institutions essential to their survival: property, customary law, and the free market.

Property for the Poor

In Peru, landless peasants had no choice but to work outside the formal state, as the famous Peruvian author Mario Vargas Llosa notes:

'When legality is a privilege available to only those with political and economic power, those excluded – the poor – have no alternative but illegality.' (de Soto, 1987, p.xii).

Through mutual co-operation, these informals, making up 48 per cent of the economically active population, have created

---

[5] In some small measure this process may already have begun: the World Development Movement, a charity, recently won a private action against Britain's Foreign Secretary, Douglas Hurd. The Judges ruled that he had acted illegally in allowing the use of ODA moneys to fund an *uneconomic* dam project in Malaysia (*The Times*, 11/11/94, pp.1-2). Section 1 of the Overseas Development and Co-operation Act 1980 states that the Foreign Secretary may only authorise aid payments 'for the purpose of promoting the development or maintaining the economy of a country or territory outside the United Kingdom, or the welfare of its people'. Given the uneconomic uses to which ODA 'aid' money has typically been put, it seems likely that most such money disbursed since 1980 has been authorised illegally.

[6] Benedict and Kerkvliet (1993) note that 'resistance comes first at the level of ideas and in small, unobtrusive ways', and later on, 'agricultural workers and peasants mobilised in large numbers on their own'. For a mathematical exposition of the evolution of revolution see Glance and Huberman (1993, 1994).

reasonably well functioning stateless societies: they produce goods and services for both the informal and the formal sectors amounting to approximately 39 per cent of Peru's annual GDP, and 90 per cent of its agricultural output (De Soto, 1987, p.12). But informality has its costs – the constant necessity of dodging the police, the lack of secure land tenure, and the difficulties of making advance arrangements when contracts are not legally enforceable.

Thus Hernando de Soto, economist, entrepreneur, and champion of the Peruvian poor, concludes (in a paragraph which would not go amiss on a future (reformed) Oxfam Campaigner newsletter):

> 'The real remedy for violence and poverty is to recognise the property and labour of those whom formality today excludes, so that where there is rebellion there will be a sense of belonging and responsibility. When people develop a taste for independence and faith in their own efforts, they will be able to believe in themselves and in economic freedom.'

Conclusions

As Mencken said, 'for every problem there is a solution that is simple, direct and wrong'. This paper does not attempt to offer such a 'solution'. But if government officials in the developed world were to stop using taxpayers' money to finance the oppressive activities of state officials in the developing world, if they were to close down the World Bank, the IMF, the United Nations and all the bilateral 'aid' organisations, and if they were to eliminate all barriers to trade,[7] the poor in the developing world would most likely all be a great deal better off.

---

[7] I make no distinction between free trade within and free trade between arbitrary political entities: the uncoerced exchange of goods between individuals is always (by definition) mutually beneficial.

7. Summary and Conclusions

This paper began with a discussion of the ideologies which have influenced the political debate over intervention in land use practices in developing countries. It was argued that the debate had concentrated on the 'scientific' identification of problems and the consequent construction of rational and 'scientific' solutions by philosopher-kings (be they Plato, colonial agriculturists, or UN officials).

In Chapter 2, evidence is presented which seems to contradict much of the 'scientific' evidence used by UN officials to justify their demands that $24 billion be spent each year for 20 years 'combating desertification'.

In Chapter 3, the scientific status of climate change predictions is called into question, and the connection between poverty, population pressure and land degradation in developing countries is contested.

Chapter 4 presents a theory of the political economy of land degradation in which individuals are assumed to act in a self-interested manner. Thus, political intervention arises not because of its tendency to promote the social good, but because of its tendency to benefit political entrepreneurs.

In Chapter 5, this model is utilised to show how political entrepreneurs have caused land degradation by distorting the incentives faced by peasants and others using the land: encouraging overuse of land by generating uncertainty over property rights (forced migration, slaughter of cattle, denial of customary tenure); underpricing agricultural output; and subsidising inappropriate agricultural inputs (fertiliser, machinery, irrigation).

Chapter 6 offers some tentative proposals for rectifying this depressing state of affairs. Key to any solution is a change in the incentives faced by (economic and political) entrepreneurs. For lobbyists in both the developed and the developing world it means being *pro* free trade and *anti* 'aid'.[1] For individuals in the developing world this means reforming or overthrowing corrupt autocratic régimes.[2]

Lobbyists should encourage state officials in both developed and developing countries to recognise the right of individuals to own property and to engage in mutually advantageous exchange.[3] As Stephan Schmidheiny (1994), founder of the World Environmental Council for Sustainable Development, puts it:

> '... efficient, transparent, reliable property rights are both an integral human right and a crucial tool in constructing this thing called sustainable development.'

However, if state officials in developed countries continue to use tax money to subsidise the activities of state officials in the developing world, no amount of good intentions will prevent the continued oppression of the majority of people in the developed world. As Sheik Muhammad Abdul, an Egyptian, said whilst on a visit to London in 1884:

> 'Do not attempt to do us any more good. Your good has done us too much harm already' (quoted by Bauer, 1982, p.86).

---

[1] Oxfam officials call for 'fair trade', but are against free trade (on the grounds that it encourages multinationals, which its officials claim are exploitative) and support 'aid' (see above). It is worth pointing out that removing 'aid' and instituting free trade would be far more likely to result in 'fair trade' (in which more of the rent from production accrues to producers) than buying a few tins of Nicaraguan coffee produced by Oxfam's favoured commune, since there would be greater competition in the intermediary markets (exporters, wholesalers and retailers), thereby reducing monopsony rents.

[2] Ayittey (1991) offers a detailed set of proposals for reforming African political and economic institutions, central to which is the reinstatement of the authority of the tribal system.

[3] Perhaps most importantly, free trade can ensure that entrepreneurs have an incentive to generate a network of supply so that, in times of drought, starvation is avoided.

Appendix

Land Degradation in the United States

As noted in Chapter 1, during the 1930s a large area of the American West suffered severe land degradation. The objectives of this Appendix are to elucidate the principal causes of this degradation, to assess the extent to which these conditions persist and to propose some reforms.

Like the deserts of Africa and Asia, the deserts of the United States owe their existence principally to climatic factors (see Chapter 2). Sheridan (1979, pp.2-3) notes that 'the Sonoran and Chihuahan deserts of the American Southwest are probably a million years old'.

The Western Range, that is the land to the West of the 100th meridian (excluding Alaska), covers an area of almost a billion acres – two-fifths of the land mass of the United States. This land is, for the most part, characterised by aridity; rainfall is scarce and unpredictable, the human population sparse (Hess, 1992). However, climate alone cannot explain the degradation of so much of the Western Range over the past century. To understand this process we must look at the ways in which the Range has been managed.

Two federal government bodies, the Bureau of Land Management (BLM) and the Forest Service, control around 315 million acres of the Western Range, where around 27,000 families make their living, grazing 7 million cattle, sheep and horses (Hess, 1992). The federal agencies, for their part, are obliged 'to create and maintain conditions under which man and nature can exist in productive harmony' (The National Environment Policy Act, 1969, cited by Hess, 1992).

Unfortunately, as Hess (1992) so eloquently shows, the reality of BLM management is very far from this idyllic vision. Indeed, the lands controlled by the BLM suffer most severely from soil erosion. This is a consequence of subsidies to grazing (by underpricing permits relative to free market levels), and to bureaucratic management which rarely coincides with the interests of the individuals affected.

Two additional federal agencies, the Bureau of Reclamation and the Army Corps of Engineers, have encouraged the overuse of water in the arid West. In their attempt to make the 'desert bloom like a rose', these bodies supplied billions of gallons of water, via giant storage and delivery projects such as the Hoover Dam and the Central Valley Project, to municipal and agricultural consumers at heavily subsidised rates (Anderson, 1983).

Summing up the evidence, Sheridan (1979, pp.121-22) blames federal subsidies for a large part of the degradation of the Western Range:

> 'The federal government subsidises both the exploitation and conservation of arid land resources. But the subsidies for conservation are meagre compared with those for exploitation. Low interest government loans for the installation of irrigation systems encourage farmers to mine groundwater. The prospect of federally financed water delivery systems encourages arid land municipalities and industries to mine groundwater as well. Federal disaster relief and commodity programs encourage arid land farmers to plow up natural grassland to plant crops such as wheat and especially cotton.'

Another culprit may also be identified: government allocation of the right to use water. During the 19th century, water rights in the arid West were defined and enforced privately on the basis of 'first in time, first in right'. However, a century of rent seeking has resulted in state ownership of water, while use rights (permits) are granted by bureaucrats. These permits specify the amount of water which may be used and the uses to which the water may be put, typically allowing the use of more water than is economically efficient, leading to excessive consumption and demands for more federally subsidised storage and delivery projects (Anderson, 1983).

The Dust Bowl of the 1930s affected most of the Great Plains, but was especially severe in the western third of Kansas, southeast Colorado, the Oklahoma Panhandle, the northeast two-thirds of the Texas Panhandle and northeast New Mexico, an area which almost exactly corresponds with the Ogallala aquifer

(Thomas & Middleton, 1994, p.21). Blame for the creation of the Dust Bowl has traditionally been placed on the switch to wheat cultivation in the 1870s combined with high wheat prices and a shift to mechanised agriculture in the 1930s (Thomas & Middleton, 1994, pp.21-23). However, the severe drought in the region from 1933 to 1938 combined with state intervention in the use of land and water must be taken into account. The drought led to desiccation of the soil, making it more susceptible to wind erosion, and meant that farmers became more reliant upon (underpriced) groundwater and water transferred from less arid areas through federally subsidised irrigation projects. If farmers had paid a market price for the water they were extracting and were free to grow the crops of their choice, the profits from wheat farming would have fallen, production would have switched to more suitable crops and the extent of wind erosion would probably have lessened significantly.

Reform of the management of the Western Range has already begun: towards the end of the 1980s, federal subsidies to storage and distribution schemes virtually dried up in the wake of budget cuts (Anderson and Leal, 1991). Further reforms are clearly desirable: the land and water of the Western Range should be privatised. Well-defined property rights, enforceable through private law and exchangeable in an unfettered free market would be most likely to resolve the problems of land degradation in the Western United States, as elsewhere.

References/Bibliography

Adams, P. (1991): *Odious Debts*, Toronto: Earthscan.

Alchian, A. (1965): 'Some Economics of Property Rights', *Il Politico*, Vol.30, pp.816-29, reprinted in Alchian, A. (1977): *Economic Forces at Work*, Indianapolis: Liberty Press.

van Andel, T.N., E. Rangjer and A. Demitrack (1990): 'Land Use and Soil Erosion in Prehistoric and Historical Greece', *Journal of Field Archeology*, Vol.17, No.4, pp.379-96.

Anderson, T.L. and P.J. Hill (1975): 'The Evolution of Property Rights: A Study of the American West', *Journal of Law and Economics*, Vol.18, pp.163-75.

Anderson, T.L. (1983) (ed.): *Water Rights: Scarce Resource Allocation, Bureaucracy, and the Environment*, San Francisco: Pacific Institute for Public Policy Research.

Anderson, T.L. and D.R. Leal (1991): *Free Market Environmentalism*, San Francisco: Pacific Research Institute for Public Policy.

Athlone (1938): 'Land Usage and Soil Erosion in Africa', A Report of the Speeches at the Dinner of the Royal African Society, 1st December 1937, supplement to the *Journal of the Royal African Society*, Vol.38, No.146.

Aubréville, A. (1949): *Climats, Forets, et Désertification de l'Afrique Tropicale*, Paris: Societé d'Editions Géographiques Maritimes et Coloniales.

Ault, D.E. and G.L. Rutman (1979): 'The Development of Individual Rights to Property in Tribal Africa', *Journal of Law and Economics*, Vol.22, pp.163-82.

Austen, R. (1987): *African Economic History*, Portsmouth: Heinemann.

Axelrod, R. (1984): *The Evolution of Co-operation*, New York: Basic Books.

Ayittey, G.B.N. (1991): *Indigenous African Institutions*, Ardsley-on-Hudson, NY: Transnational Publishers.

_____ (1992): *Africa Betrayed*, Washington, DC: Cato Institute.

Balling, R. (1992): *The Heated Debate: Greenhouse Predictions versus Climate Reality*, San Francisco: Pacific Research Institute for Public Policy.

Balling, R.C. (1991): 'Impact of Desertification on Regional and Global Warming', *Bulletin of the American Meteorological Society*, Vol.72, pp.232-34.

Bandow, D. and I. Vasquez (1994): *Perpetuating Poverty*, Wahington, DC: Cato Institute.

Barrett, J. (1995): 'The Rôles of Carbon Dioxide and Water Vapour in Warming and Cooling the Earth's Troposphere', *Spectrochemica Acta*.

Bate, R. and J. Morris (1994): *Global Warming: Apocalypse or Hot Air?*, IEA Studies on the Environment No.1, London: Institute of Economic Affairs.

Bates, R. (1984): *Essays on the Political Economy of Africa*, Cambridge: Cambridge University Press.

Bauer, P.T. (1982): *Equality, The Third World and Economic Delusion*, London: Methuen.

Benedict, J. and T. Kirkvliet (1993): 'Claiming the Land: Take-overs by Villagers in the Philippines with Comparisons to Indonesia, Peru, Portugal and Russia', *Journal of Peasant Studies*, Vol.20, pp.459-93.

Benson, B. (1990): *The Enterprise of Law*, San Francisco: Pacific Research Institute for Public Policy.

Berman, H. (1982): *Law and Revolution*, Cambridge, MA: Harvard University Press.

Bernstam, M.S. (1991): *The Wealth of Nations and the Environment*, Occasional Paper No.85, London: Institute of Economic Affairs.

Blackwell, J.M., R.N. Goodwillie and R. Webb (1991): 'Environment and Development in Africa – Selected Case Studies', Economic Development Institute of The World Bank, *EDI Development Policy Case Studies Series, Analytical Case Studies Number 6*.

Boserup, E. (1988): 'Environment, Population and Technology in Primitive Societies', in D. Worster (ed.), *The Ends of The Earth*, Cambridge: Cambridge University Press.

Bottcher, C.J.F. (1992): *Science and Fiction of the Greenhouse Effect and Carbon Dioxide*, The Hague, The Netherlands: Global Institute for the Study of Natural Resources.

Boulding, K. (1966): *The Economics of the Coming Spaceship Earth*, reprinted in De Bell (1970), pp.96-101.

Bovill, E.W. (1921): 'The encroachment of the Sahara on the Sudan', *Journal of the Royal African Society*, Vol.20 (175-185), pp.259-69.

Bromley, D. (1991): *Environment and Economy*, Oxford: Basil Blackwell.

Brookfield, H. and C. Padoch (1994): 'Appreciating Agro-diversity', *Environment*, Vol.36, No.5, June, pp.6-11, 37-45.

Buchanan, J.M. and G. Tullock (1962): *The Calculus of Consent*, Ann Arbor,MI: Michigan University Press.

Buchanan, J.M. (1965): 'An Economic Theory of Clubs', *Economica*, Vol.32, pp.1-14.

Burton, J. (1978): 'Epilogue: Externalities, Property Rights and Public Policy: Private Property Rights or the Spoilation of Nature', in Cheung (1978).

Chamlee, E. (1993): 'Indigenous African Institutions and Economic Development', *Cato Journal*, Vol.13, pp.79-99.

Cheung, S.N.S. (1978): *The Myth of Social Cost*, Hobart Paper No. 82, London: Institute of Economic Affairs.

Cooke, R., A. Warren and A. Goudie (1993): *Desert Geomorphology*, London: UCL Press.

Council on Environmental Quality (CEQ) (1986): *Environmental Quality 1985, 16th Annual Report of the Council on Environmental Quality*, Washington, DC: CEQ.

Cowen, T. (1992): *Public Goods and Market Failures*, New Brunswick: Transactions Press.

Darling, P.D. (1993): 'Updating Some African Population Myths', Paper for the First World Optimum Population Congress, 8-11 August.

Dawkins, R. (1989): *The Selfish Gene*, 2nd Edn., Oxford: Oxford University Press.

De Bell, E. (ed.) (1970): *The Environmental Handbook*, Prepared for the First National Environmental Teach In, New York: Ballantine/Friends of the Earth.

Demsetz, H. (1967): 'Toward a Theory of Property Rights', *American Economic Review*, Vol.57, pp.347-59.

Diamond, L. (1988): *Democracy in Developing Countries: Africa*, Boulder: Lynne Reiner Publishers.

Dolan, E.G. (1974): 'Environmental Policy and Property Rights', in S. Blumfield (ed.), *Property in a Humane Economy*, Lasalle: Open Court/Institute for Humane Studies.

Dregne, H.E., M. Kassas and B. Rozanov (1991): 'A New Assessment of the World Status of Desertification', *Desertification Control Bulletin*, No.20, pp.7-18.

Dregne, H.E., and C.J. Tucker (1988): 'Desert Encroachment', *Desertification Control Bulletin*, No.16, pp.16-19.

Eberstadt, N. (1994): 'Population, Food and Income: Global Trends in the Twentieth Century', mimeo, Washington DC: The Competitive Enterprise Institute.

Eberstadt, N. (1995): 'Population, Food, and Income: Global Trends in the Twentieth Century', in R. Bailey (ed.), *The True State of The Planet*, New York: The Free Press.

Ellickson, R. (1991): *Order Without Law*, Cambridge, MA: Harvard University Press.

Fieldhouse, D. (1986): *Black Africa 1945-1980*, London: Allen and Unwin.

Foldvary, F. (1994): *Private Provision of Public Goods*, Fairfax: The Locke Institute/Edward Elgar.

Forse, B. (1989): 'The Myth of the Marching Sands', *New Scientist*, February, pp.31-2.

Fratkin, E. (1991): *Surviving Drought and Development – Ariaal Pastoralists of Northern Kenya*, Boulder: Westview Press.

GAP II (1990): 'UNEP Global Assessment of Land Degradation/Desertification – GAP II', *Desertification Control Bulletin*, No.18, pp.24-5.

Gellar, S. (1973): 'State-Building and Nation-Building in West Africa', in S.N. Eisenstadt and S. Rokkan (eds.), *Building States and Nations: Models, Analyses, and Data across Three Worlds*, Vol.2, pp.384-426, Beverly Hills: Sage.

_____ (1986): 'The Colonial State', in Martin and O'Meara (1986), pp.122-40.

Gibbon, P. (1992): 'A Failed Agenda? African Agriculture Under Structural Adjustment with Special Reference to Kenya and Ghana', *Journal of Peasant Studies*, Vol.20, pp.50-96.

Glance, N.S. and B.A. Huberman (1993): 'The Outbreak of Cooperation', *Journal of Mathematical Sociology*, Vol.17, pp.281-302.

_____ (1994): 'The Dynamics of Social Dilemmas', *Scientific American*, March, pp.58-63.

Glantz, M.H. and N. Orlovsky (1984): 'Desertification: A Review of the Concept', *Desertification Control Bulletin*, pp.15-22.

Goodell, G., *The Philippines*, in Powelson and Stock (1990), pp.15-34.

Hancock, G. (1989): *The Lords of Poverty*, London: Macmillan; New York: Atlantic Monthly Press.

Hardin, G. (1968): 'The Tragedy of the Commons', *Science*, Vol.62, 13 December, pp.1,243-48.

Harrison, P. (1989): *The Greening of Africa*, London: Paladin.

Hayek, F.A. (1945): 'The Use of Knowledge in Society', *American Economic Review*, Vol.35, pp.519-30.

Helldén, U. (1984): 'Drought Impact Monitoring: A Remote Sensing Study of Desertification in Kordofan, Sudan', *Rapporter och Notiser*, Vol.61, Lunds Universitets Naturgeografiska Institution.

_____ (1988): 'Desertification Monitoring: Is the Desert Encroaching?', *Desertification Control Bulletin*, Vol.17, pp.8-12.

_____ (1991): 'Desertification: Time for an Assessment?', *Ambio*, Vol.20, No.8, pp.372-83.

Hess Jr., K. (1992): *Visions Upon The Land: Man and Nature on the Western Range*, Washington, DC: Island Press.

Hirschman, A. (1970): *Exit, Voice and Loyalty*, Cambridge, MA: Harvard University Press.

Hobbes, T. (1649/1991): *Leviathan*, Cambridge: Cambridge University Press.

Idso, S.B. (1991): 'The Aerial Fertilization Effect of CO_2 and its Implications for the Global Carbon Cycling and Maximum Greenhouse Warming', *Bulletin of the American Meteorological Association*, Vol.72, pp.962-5.

Independent Commission on International Humanitarian Issues (ICIHI) (1986): *The Encroaching Desert: The Consequences of Human Failure*, London: Zed Books.

IPCC (1990): First Report of the Intergovernmental Panel on Climate Change, Cambridge: Cambridge University Press.

_____ (1992): Second Report of the Intergovernmental Panel on Climate Change, Cambridge: Cambridge University Press.

Jackson, R.H. and C.G. Rosberg (1982): *Personal Rule in Black Africa: Prince, Autocrat, Prophet, Tyrant*, Berkeley: University of California Press.

de Jasay, A. (1989): *Social Contract, Free Ride*, Oxford: Oxford University Press.

Johnson, P. (1993): 'The Earth Summit', *The United Nations Conference on Environment and Development (UNCED)*, London: Graham and Trotman/Martinus Nijhoff.

Kasun, J. (1988): *The War Against Population: The Economics and Ideology of Population Control*, San Francisco: Ignatius.

Kassas, M., Y.J. Ahmad and B. Rozanov (1991): 'Desertification and Drought: An Ecological and Economic Analysis', *Desertification Control Bulletin*, No.20, pp.19-29.

Krueger, A.O. (1974): 'The Political Economy of the Rent-Seeking Society', *American Economic Review*, Vol.64, pp.291 -303.

Lamb, H.H. (1974): 'The Earth's Changing Climate', *The Ecologist*, Vol.4, pp.10-15.

Lamprey, H.F. (1988): 'Report on the Desert Encroachment Reconnaissance in Northern Sudan, 21 October to 10 November 1975', *Desertification Control Bulletin*, No.17, pp.1-7.

Larson, B.A. (1994): 'Changing the Economics of Environmental Degradation in Madagascar: Lessons from the National Environmental Action Plan [NEAP] Process', *World Development*, Vol.22, No.5, pp.671-89.

Livingstone, D. (1857): *Missionary Travels and Researches in South Africa*, London: J. Murray.

Luow, L. and F. Kendall (1986): *South Africa: The Solution*, Bisho, Ciskei: Amigi Publications.

Mabbutt, J.A. (1984): 'A New Global Assessment of the Status and Trends of Desertification', *Environmental Conservation*, Vol.11, pp.103-13.

Mahmood, K. (1987): 'Reservoir Sedimentation: Impact, Extent, and Mitigation', *World Bank Technical Paper*, No.71, Washington, DC: The World Bank.

Malthus, T.R. (1798/1976): *An Essay Concerning the Principle of Population*, P. Appleman (ed.), New York: W.W. Norton.

Manning, Patrick (1988): *Francophone Sub-Saharan Africa 1880-1985*, Cambridge: Cambridge University Press.

Martin, P.M. and P. O'Meara (eds.) (1986): *Africa*, Bloomington: Indiana University Press.

Mbaku, J. (1991): 'Property Rights and Rent Seeking in South Africa', *Cato Journal*, Vol.11, pp.135-50.

Mbaku, J. and C. Paul (1989): 'Political Instability in Africa: A Rent-Seeking Approach', *Public Choice*, Vol.63, pp.63-72.

Meissalloux, C. (1962): 'Social and Economic Factors Affecting Markets in Guru Land', in P. Bohanon and G. Dalton (eds.), *Markets in Africa*, Evanston: Northwestern University Press.

Michaels, P.J. (1992): *Sound and Fury: The Science and Politics of Global Warming*, Washington, DC: Cato Institute.

Middleton, N.J. and D.S.G. Thomas (1992): *World Atlas of Desertification*, Sevenoaks: Edward Arnold/ UNEP.

von Mises, L. (1951): *Socialism*, 2nd Edn., New Haven: Yale University Press.

Monbiot, G. (1994): 'The Tragedy of Enclosure', *Scientific American*, January, p.140.

Mortimore, M. (1990): *Adapting to Drought: Farmers, Famines and Desertification in West Africa*, Cambridge: Cambridge University Press.

Nelson, R. (1990): 'Dryland Management: The "Desertification Problem"', *World Bank Technical Paper*, No.116, Washington, DC: The World Bank.

Nettl, J.P. and R. Robertson (1968): *International Systems and the Modernisation of Society*, London: Faber.

Nkrumah, K. (1973): *Revolutionary Path*, New York: International Publishers.

Northrup, D. (1978): *Trade Without Rulers: Pre-Colonial Economic Development in South-Eastern Nigeria*, Oxford: Clarendon.

Odingo, R.S. (1990): 'The Definition of Desertification: Its Programmatic Consequences for UNEP and the International Community', *Desertification Bulletin*, No.18, pp.31-50.

_____ (1992): 'Implementation of the Plan of Action to Combat Desertification (PACD) 1978-1991', *Desertification Control Bulletin*, No.21, pp.6-14.

Operations Evaluations Department (1989): 'Renewable Resource Management in Agriculture', *World Bank Operations Evaluations Study*, Washington, DC: IBRD.

Ostrom, E. (1988): 'Institutional Arrangements and the Commons Dilemma', in V. Ostrom *et al.* (1988), pp.101-39.

_____ (1990): *Managing the Commons*, Cambridge: Cambridge University Press.

Ostrom, V., D. Feeny and H. Picht (eds.) (1988): *Rethinking Institutional Analysis and Development*, San Francisco: ICS Press.

Pakenham, T. (1991): *The Scramble for Africa*, London: Wiedenfeld and Nicolson.

Pearce, F. (1992): 'Mirage of the Shifting Sands', *New Scientist*, 12 December.

Pejovitch, S. (1972): 'Towards an Economic Theory of the Creation and Enforcement of Property Rights', *Review of Social Economics*.

Plato (1955): *The Republic*, D. Lee (ed.), London: Penguin Books.

Powelson, J. and R. Stock (1990): *The Peasant Betrayed*, Washington, DC: Cato Institute.

Pritchett, L.H. and L.H. Summers (1994): 'Desired Fertility and the Impact of Population Policies', *World Bank Policy Research Working Papers*, No.1,273, March.

Rich, B. (1994): *Mortgaging the Earth*, London: Earthscan.

Rozanov, B. (1990): *Global assessment of desertification: Status and Methodologies*, in UNEP-DC/PAC.

Sachs, J. (1994): 'Beyond Bretton Woods', *The Economist*, 1-7 October.

Sawyer, A. (1988): 'The Development of Autocracy in Liberia', in Ostrom *et al.* (1988).

Samuelson, P. (1954): 'The Pure Theory of Public Expenditure', *Review of Economics and Statistics*, No.36, pp.387-89.

Schechter, J. (1977): 'Desertification Processes and the Search for Solutions', *Interdisciplinary Science Reviews*, Vol.2, No.1, pp.36-54.

Schlager, E. and E. Ostrom (1992): 'Property-Rights Régimes and Natural Resources: A Conceptual Analysis', *Land Economics*, Vol.68, pp.249-62.

Schmidheiny, S. (1994): 'Property Rights and Sustainable Development', in *Property for the Poor: The Path to Development*, proceedings of a conference organised by the Institute for Liberty and Democracy, 12 April, Washington, DC.

Schneider, H.K. (1986): 'Traditional African Economies', in P.M. Martin and P. O'Meara (eds.), *Africa*, Bloomington: Indiana University Press.

Schneider, S.H., P.H. Gleick, and L.O. Mearns, (1990): 'Prospects of Climate Change', in P.E. Waggoner (ed.), *Climate Change and US Water Resources*, New York: Wiley.

Schumpeter, J.A. (1954): *A History of Economic Analysis*, London: Allen & Unwin.

Schwartz, E.H.L. (1919): 'The Progressive Desiccation of Africa: The Cause and the Remedy', *South African Journal of Science*, Vol.15, pp.139-90.

_____ (1921): *The Kalahari or Thirstland Redemption*, Cape Town: Masker Miller.

Sheridan, D. (1981): *Desertification of the United States*, Washington, DC: Council on Environmental Quality.

Smith, A. (1776): *An Inquiry into the Nature and Causes of the Wealth of Nations,* ed. Edwin Cannan, Chicago: University of Chicago Press, 1976.

SOS Sahel (1992): *At the Desert's Edge: Oral Histories from the Sahel*, London: Panos.

de Soto, H. (1989): *The Other Path: The Invisible Revolution in the Third World*, New York: Harper and Row.

Stahl, M. (1993): 'Land Degradation in East Africa', *Ambio*, Vol.22, No.8, December, pp.505-8.

Stebbing, E.P. (1935): 'The Encroaching Sahara: The Threat to the West African Colonies', *Geographical Journal*, Vol.85, p.506.

Sugden, R. (1986): *The Economics of Rights, Co-operation and Welfare*, Oxford: Basil Blackwell.

Suliman, M.M. (1988): 'Dynamics of Range Plants and Desertification Monitoring in the Sudan', *Desertification Control Bulletin*, No.16, pp.27-31.

Thomas, D.S.G. and N.J. Middleton (1994): *Desertification: Exploding the Myth*, London: Wiley.

Tiffen, M., M. Mortimore and F. Gichuki (1994): *More People, Less Erosion: Environmental Recovery in Kenya*, Chichester: John Wiley and Sons.

Tucker, C.J., H.E. Dregne and W.W. Newcombe (1991): 'Expansion and Contraction of the Sahara Desert from 1980 to 1990', *Science*, Vol.253, pp.299-301.

Tullock, G. (1967): 'The Welfare Costs of Tariffs, Monopolies and Theft', *Western Economic Journal*, Vol.5, pp.224-32.

_____ (1987): *Autocracy*, Boston: Kluwer Academic Publishers.

_____ (1993): *Rent Seeking*, Fairfax: The Locke Institute.

Turke, P.W. (1989): 'Evolution and the Demand for Children', *Population and Development Review*, Vol.15, pp.61-90.

Umali, D.L. (1993): 'Irrigation-Induced Salinity: A Growing Problem for Development and the Environment', *World Bank Technical Paper*, No.215.

UNEP DC/PAC (1984): *Activities of the United Nations Environment Programme in the Combat Against Desertification*, Nairobi: UNEP.

_____ (1990): *Desertification Revisited: Proceedings of an Ad Hoc Consultative Meeting on the Assessment of Desertification*, Nairobi: UNEP.

UN General Assembly (1994): United Nations Convention to Combat Desertification in Countries Experiencing Serious Drought and/or Desertification, Particularly in Africa, (A/AC.241/27), 12 September, Chatelaine, Switzerland.

UNSO (1990): 'United Nations Sudano-Sahelian Office', *Desertification Bulletin*, No.18, p.30.

USAID (1972): 'Desert Encroachment on Arable Lands', Office of Science and Technology, Washington, DC: Agency for International Development.

US Government Document NSSM 200 (1974): 'Implications of Worldwide Population Growth for US Security and Overseas Interests', 10 December, cited by Kasun (1988), p.199.

Wade, N. (1974): 'Sahelian Drought: No Victory for Western Aid', *Science*, Vol.185, 19 July, pp.234-37.

Wall, D. (ed.) (1994): *Green History*, London: Routledge.

Walters, A. (1994): *Do We Need the IMF and the World Bank?*, IEA Current Controversies No.10, London: IEA.

Warren, A. and C.T. Agnew (1988): 'An Assessment of Desertification and Land Degradation in Arid and Semi-Arid Areas', *Report for Greenpeace International, also in International Institute for Environment and Development* (IIED) Paper No.2 (1988).

Warren, A. and M. Khogali (1992): *Assessment of Desertification and Drought in the Sudano-Sahelian Region, 1985-1991*, UNDP/UNSO.

Whitaker, J.S. (1988): *How Can Africa Survive?*, New York: Harper and Row.

Zolberg, A.R. (1966): *Creating Political Order: The Party-States of West Africa*, Chicago: Rand McNally.